TERMS OF ENGAGEMENT

CHANGING THE WAY
WE CHANGE ORGANIZATIONS

RICHARD H. AXELROD

BERRETT-KOEHLER PUBLISHERS, INC.
San Francisco

Berrett-Koehler Publishers, Inc.
450 Sansome Street, Suite 1200
San Francisco, CA 94111-3320
Tel: (415) 288-0260   Fax: (415) 362-2512
www.bkconnection.com

The Conference Model is a registered trademark of The Axelrod Group, Inc.

ORDERING INFORMATION

Individual sales. Berrett-Koehler publications are available through most bookstores.
They can also be ordered direct from Berrett-Koehler at the address above.

Quantity sales. Special discounts are available on quantity purchases by corporations,
associations, and others. For details, contact the "Special Sales Department" at the
Berrett-Koehler address above.

Orders for college textbook/course adoption use. Please contact Berrett-Koehler
Publishers at the address above.

Orders by U.S. trade bookstores and wholesalers. Please contact Publishers Group West,
1700 Fourth Street, Berkeley, CA 94710. Tel: 510-528-1444; Fax: 510-528-3444.

Printed in the United States of America
Printed on acid-free and recycled paper that is composed of 50% recycled fiber,
including 10% postconsumer waste.

Library of Congress Cataloging-in-Publication Data

Axelrod, Richard H., 1943-
    Terms of engagement : changing the way we change organizations / by Richard H.
Axelrod.— 1st ed.
        p. cm.
    Includes bibliographical references and index.
    ISBN 1-57675-084-1
    1. Organizational change—Management. 2. Employee motivation. I. Title.

    HF58.8 .A94 2000
    658.4'06—dc21
                                                                        99-044009

First Edition

04 03 02 01 00   10 9 8 7 6 5 4 3 2 1

Book Production: Pleasant Run Publishing Services
Composition: Classic Typography

To my parents
Sidney and Carolyn

Contents

PART 1
The Problem and the Solution

PART 2
Producing the Engaged Organization

PART 3
Getting Started

Foreword
The Means of Engagement

We put great energy into trying to change our organizations and it is always more difficult and takes longer than we imagined. Some of this is in the nature of change and the general human reluctance to give up a known though painful present for an unknown though possible future. Much of the resistance to change, however, grows out of the way we try to achieve it. Often I think that people are not so much resistant to change, which happens all the time, as we are resistant to imposition and to persuasive, new-age coercion.

The most common way we try to change organizations is through strong leadership, clear vision, enrollment, rewards, and training events designed to get the new message across. Leaders and their specialists huddle to devise strategies to get employees, customers, and the universal targets of change—the stakeholders—"on board." Those planning the change somehow think that it is they who are in the boat and others who are in the water. When people talk of the need for change, they are usually thinking that it is someone else who needs to change.

This mind-set is what drives modern change management methods that include many meetings, many presentations, endless discussions of burning platform issues, lots of process-improvement programs, and a basket of essentially leader-directed moves. And when the change process is too slow, the typical response is to redouble our efforts and drive faster. As if picking up speed will solve the problem of being on the wrong road. In some ways it may help, for we are able to get to the wrong destination faster.

The alternative to leader-driven change and leader-driven meetings held to drive the change is to explore the possibility of engagement, relationship, and democracy as the methodology that will get us to the right place. That is what this book is about. The tools and strategy of engagement. Innovative ways to mobilize human energy in service of the institution or community.

The uniqueness of this book is its concreteness and its lovingly democratic values. It is very specific and creative about the choreography of how to bring people together, not to dance or to socialize, but to get something done. If you watched a change or learning effort take place, you would not observe minds whirling, what you would observe is people meeting with each other. We need a rational strategy, clear vision, and good information, but it comes into use when we talk about it. If you are interested, then, in how change and learning really takes place, you end up designing meetings. Who should be in the room, how should we seat them and group them, what is the conversation people ought to be having?

The way we bring people together, then, becomes a major concern for how change happens. We live in a culture that believes that the way to plan a meeting to gain support for new ideas is to make a strong case, present it well, and ask for people's commitment. It is basically a selling strategy. If you look at the way we meet in organizations and communities across the country, you see a lot of presenters, a lot of podiums, and a lot of passive audiences. This reflects our naïveté in how to bring people together.

Also, when we do search for new ways to structure a gathering, we relegate the question to facilitators and process specialists. Too often we think it is a third party's job to worry about the people side of a gathering, it is the manager's job to give attention to what we want to present to each other. We act as if "process" and "content" are somehow separate questions, and often at odds with each other. Even then, if you simply measure the amount of time devoted to content and process in each planning and strategy activity, "content" wins without a contest. A good group process is needed whenever two or two hundred people meet, and the tension between process and content is a fool's dilemma. There is no need to choose between the two—both are essential, they fail without each other.

The time is right for a book on how to bring people together in a way that defines a change strategy based on genuine participation and human interaction. And we need a book that is written not for specialists but for managers and staff people who need a good group process and yet do not think of it as their life work. How we come together, which is here labeled engagement, is everybody's task, every time we meet, and the conventional wisdom about how to manage a meeting is in serious need of updating.

Many of our conventional ideas about gatherings find root in the beliefs of one Henry Martyn Robert and his rules. Robert was a Civil War military engineer who grew frustrated with the lack of productivity he encountered in community work after the war and he published a pamphlet about how to get things done in meetings. It went unnoticed until the turn of the century when a publishing house picked it up and it got wide distribution. Now *Robert's Rules of Order*, or its grandchildren, invade every conference room and meeting hall. There is no escape.

The contribution of *Robert's Rules* is the importance the book gives to the question of group process. The downside of the rules is the essentially legislative solution they offer to meetings and the way they promote the thinking that control and predictability are the keys to success. Even though, in most work settings, we do not follow the rules explicitly, the belief that meetings should be engineered for efficiency is still very much with us. We have this image that a good meeting is one where the presentation is clear and power pointed, things move quickly, there is little conflict and we don't waste time with feelings. This is the industrial model of relationships.

We need to amend this worship of efficiency. Workplaces and communities are human systems. Human systems require patience, they grow out of conflict, and succeed when feelings are connected to purpose. Meetings have a deeper meaning than just to cover the content and decide something. Meetings are an important place where commitments and relationships are either chosen or denied. Every change effort holds a meeting at some early point to move the change forward, and it is often the experience we have in that meeting that influences whether we decide to commit to the change or simply give it lip service.

What is missing in the consciousness of many managers is the reality that the social structure of how we come together determines the real, human outcome of the event. You can not have a high control, leader-driven meeting to introduce a high involvement, high commitment change effort. High control, efficient ways of coming together, symbolized by Robert's Rules and "good presentation skills," sacrifice the opportunity for relationships to be built both between employees and their leaders and employees with each other. If you want change to be supported, even embraced, you focus less on charisma, rewards and motivators and more on honest conversation, high involvement and strong, high-trust relationships.

A meeting also has a symbolic significance over and above the specific content it was called for. It is much like the meaning dinnertime has for our experience of the family (on those occasions when we eat together). It is when all of us are at the dinner table together that we get a sense of the whole. It is the moment we are physically reminded that we are a part of something larger. When we are on our own, we know intellectually we are a part of a larger something, but it is a thought, not an experience. At the dinner table, we get a concrete, visceral picture of what the place is like and how it is doing. Whether the meal becomes a warm conversation or a food fight, we still get the picture. The family dynamics and culture become visible at these moments. And if we no longer all come together for a meal, that too becomes a measure of our isolation and separate ways.

Same with an organization's culture. It becomes visible and is open to influence when groups of people are gathered in the same room. It doesn't matter whether we come together to get information, learn something or are trying to decide something. The structure, aliveness, deadness, whisper or shout of the meeting teaches and persuades us more about the culture of our workplace than all the speeches about core values and the new culture we are striving for.

This is why meetings are important. The experience of the meeting carries the message of the culture and most critically, it is the quality of this experience that determines whether people leave the meeting with optimism and a genuine desire to make something happen. Even using the term "meeting" understates the importance of when and how we come together. What we call "meetings" are critical cultural passages that in each case, create an opportunity for connection and the kind of engagement that this book is about.

It is right, then, to equate engagement with change. Each time we come together, whether it is a conference, a training session, a public hearing or a large group meeting of employees, there is the opportunity to create a culture of openness, relationship and trust in leadership. If these gatherings are done in a way that evokes people's optimism and trust in their environment, then whatever the content of the meeting, the participants will leave more committed and willing to invest than when they arrived.

If you are in the business of attempting to shift a culture or change the direction of the organization, then your methods of engagement will be the vehicle to make this happen. This is why this book is important.

This book, as a reflection of Dick and Emily's work over the last ten years, offers the specifics of how engagement strategies can work. If we have held onto leader-driven and directive strategies too long because we do not know what the alternative is or how to implement it, then these questions are answered in the book. After you read this book, you will no longer have the excuse that we sustain leader-driven, directed change because we do not know what else to do. If you really believe that instead of engagement, stronger drivers are needed to reach your destination, then you had best not read the book. Better to be accused of innocence than negligence.

Regardless of your own philosophy of change, read the book and enjoy it. It is a much broader statement than simply how to bring people together. It positions engagement as a cornerstone to our future and gives every manager and staff person the skills and concepts that until now have resided primarily in the hands of facilitators and consultants. The Bible can now be read by lay men and women, and in this intention, it is much needed and gently revolutionary.

Peter Block

Preface

Terms of Engagement: Changing the Way We Change Organizations represents a lifetime of work in American business. Although I did not realize it when I began to write, my whole life—from my very first work experiences in my father's factory through my management today of my own consulting company—has been a preparation for this book. For more than forty years, I have watched leaders use everything from command-and-control techniques to highly participative practices to effect change in their organizations, and I have concluded that, without engagement, no lasting change is possible.

I worked in my father's model airplane factory on weekends and every summer from the time I was fourteen years old until I graduated from college. In my earliest jobs at the factory, I drifted through each day without any sense of engagement in what I was doing. As a machinist's helper, I learned to put tools back in their exact place, not one centimeter to the right or left. I experienced the joy of sweeping clean floors so they would be cleaner. I learned what it is like to live from break to break, your life governed by the clock. I learned what it is like to be unengaged.

A few years later, I was given jobs where time flew by and the clock was irrelevant, jobs that gave me responsibility and challenged me to think. One summer, I ran the shipping department and learned the intricacies of working with truckers, shippers, and an alcoholic freight-elevator operator. Another year, I worked in the front office and learned the importance of cost accounting and inventory control. I also worked on special projects to improve productivity and yield. Through these experiences, I learned about the creative spirit that existed within me and within all my coworkers who had ideas about how to make things easier and better.

Throughout these years, I was in the unique position of being privy both to my father's musings about how to motivate the workforce and to my coworkers' frequent indifference to his attempts. There is nothing like seeing your father's name in graffiti on bathroom walls to make you realize something is wrong. In short, as I began to observe what worked and what did not, the seeds of my life's work were planted.

In college, not surprisingly, I studied industrial management. A crisis occurred for me in a class on time and motion studies. As the professor droned on about motivation and incentive piece rates, characterizing human beings solely as economic commodities, I felt as if I were listening to someone from another planet. I recalled my experience working on the line and knew that his thinking was shallow, primitive, and even dangerous. His Pavlovian notions about motivation did not take into account the creativity and ingenuity I had encountered daily.

In the military, as a young second lieutenant, a single incident taught me that leadership is more than giving orders. One morning during officer training, I and the other members of my squad were being led by someone we did not respect. There was grumbling in the ranks as he strode toward us, and when he shouted, "Follow me," no one moved. We were making a statement: we would not follow orders from someone we did not respect. I learned that officers had the power to give orders, but that enlisted personnel had the power to choose how such orders were carried out. Orders could be carried out to their full intent, or not at all.

It was also in the military that I first learned about the need for planning and for managing transitions. I was assigned the responsibility of moving a radio station and, thinking it would be a piece of cake, I gave little thought to the need for planning each step of the move and creating backup systems to take over during the transition. Consequently, a job I thought would take no more than four hours took two days, and the radio station was off the air for eight hours! The next day, the battalion commander forever imprinted on my psyche the need to devise a comprehensive plan and to anticipate transitions.

When I left the military, I took a job as manager of repair service at a telephone company. There, I experienced what happens when you engage people deeply in change. I was fortunate enough to participate in some early experiments in organizational development in the Bell system to study the impact of using survey-guided development and team development to improve service quality and productivity. Within a year, our unit's results increased from average to first or second in every measurable category. In addition, every day we put eighty-five trucks on the Chicago streets, and our unit did not have any traffic accidents for an entire year. We did not increase the number of safety lectures or demonstrations. Instead, we changed the relationship between the supervisor and the crew. Supervisors increased the involvement of their crews in planning workloads and decision making.

In 1981, I formed the Axelrod Group and began consulting to industry. During this time, our primary method for bringing about organizational change was through the parallel organization, the foundation of the current change management paradigm. But in the late 1980s, my colleagues and I began to realize that there was something terribly wrong with this approach to change. Although it was better than previous approaches, it took too long and did not sufficiently engage the organization. Thus meaningful, lasting change did not occur. For a while, we tinkered with this paradigm, adjusting first one aspect then another to no avail. It was time for a totally new approach.

In 1991, we developed the Conference Model, a radically new approach to organizational redesign. The Conference Model process engaged large numbers of people in the redesign of their organizations through a series of conferences (two- or three-day workshops) and walkthrus (smaller sessions involving those not present at the conferences). The results were astounding: we were able to engage more people in the process, to move more quickly from planning to implementation, and to produce meaningful, lasting change because we had created a critical mass of people who were invested in the outcomes.

Our thinking has matured and developed since the early days of the Conference Model. In the beginning, we focused on getting the techniques right. Now our attention has shifted to the principles behind the techniques. Taken together, these principles constitute the *engagement paradigm,* our system for exploring the question of how to engage people in meaningful, lasting change, and—an even larger question—how to produce an engaged organization.

In 1992, an event in my personal life taught me more about change than I'd learned in twenty-five years of consulting to businesses. That year, I had emergency triple-bypass surgery and spent twenty days in the hospital because of surgical complications. Having your chest cracked open is a life-changing event, one I do not wish to repeat. As a result, I decided to change my lifestyle radically. I became a vegetarian, limited my fat intake to 10 percent, and added aerobic exercise and yoga to my life on a daily basis.

My engagement with this lifestyle change has ebbed and flowed. Sometimes, it feels effortless. Other times, it seems to be more than I can handle. At times, I care about it deeply. But some days, I feel doubtful or even indifferent. For instance, there is nothing more basic than changing the way you eat. Removing all animal products from your diet sets you apart. Every meal becomes an exercise in decision making, and dining out tests your assertiveness. Though I have rarely cheated on my diet, I have complained about it and sometimes doubted its merits. Whenever I do so, I am amazed to recognize that, even with years of experience in leading change efforts, even when the stakes are completely personal and very high—when one's very life is at stake—engagement does not come easily. Going through this change process, observing my own engagement with it, has given me new insights, patience, and understanding about change processes in general.

And so I welcome you to explore with me the challenges and rewards of *Terms of Engagement.* My profound hope is that reading this book will cause you to think about, design, and implement change in a new way. After all, that is what paradigm shifts are all about.

Acknowledgments

For believing in this book when it was just an idea, my colleague and friend Peter Block and my agent Sheryl Fullerton, and to Steve Piersanti at Berrett-Koehler for teaching me the meaning of profound simplicity.

Every writer needs a coach and a great editor. Thanks to Richard Ogle for seeing in me the possibilities that I did not see in myself and to Laura Bonazzoli and Hilary Powers for editing with skill, sensitivity, and tact.

To my colleagues at The Axelrod Group for your support and encouragement over the years, Steve Treacy, Nancy Voss, Rosemarie Barbeau, Diane Franz. And for their work on the manuscript, special thanks to Rachel Singer and Rachel Nyanya. To Lois Welch, thanks for your support and interest. Moreover, thanks to Julie Beedon from Vista Consulting for great conversations and insights from across the pond.

Thanks to all those who shared their stories and experiences, especially Lisa MacPherson, Nancy Aronson, Beverly Arsht, Jolene Tornabeni, Mary Jane Mastorovich, Alan Davies, Neil Watson, Kate Nash, June Gunter, Weldon Rucker, Jonelle Adams, Neil Robertson, and John Bradberry.

To the clients of the Axelrod Group, thanks for allowing us the privilege of working with you.

To my family for their support and encouragement, particularly Heather and David, my daughter and son, for reading drafts and providing the constructive criticism that only family members can provide and for just asking, "Hey Dad, how's the book coming along?"

To Emily, my wife and partner for over thirty years, thanks for being Emily.

March 2000   Richard H. Axelrod
Wilmette, Illinois

Introduction
You Can't Get There Alone

In today's business world, it sometimes seems as if everything is changing at the speed of light. Rapidly changing technology makes yesterday's innovative ideas obsolete. There is more access to information today than in the whole history of civilization, yet people are increasingly lonely, isolated, and disconnected. Extreme wealth and poverty live side by side while the gap between them increases exponentially. Organizations find themselves existing simultaneously as competitors and partners. Mergers and acquisitions are occurring so fast that it is almost impossible to keep track of the names of the new entities. Globalization requires organizations to overcome the barriers of language, culture, time, and distance. There is rising authoritarianism as leaders attempt to control the chaos. The changes are so profound and occurring so rapidly that we often experience them as a dizzying blur. Yet this is our reality, and in this world success belongs to those organizations that are able to respond effectively to this increasingly complex, turbulent environment.

Unfortunately, the approach to organizational change employed by most organizations and consulting firms—what I am calling the change management paradigm—is inadequate for today's world. When speed and agility are essential, it provides a sluggish bureaucratic response. When creativity is essential, it thwarts innovation, adaptation, and learning. Worse yet, instead of creating true ownership, commitment, and a critical mass of people who care about the outcomes, the change management paradigm actually increases bureaucracy and reinforces top-down management, while increasing cynicism and resistance in the workforce.

In a time when the world was more stable and the pace of change was slower, this once-revolutionary practice successfully introduced new levels of employee participation and helped organizations change. In the 1980s, many leading organizations such as Ford Motor Company used this paradigm to successfully improve productivity and quality. However, the change management paradigm has lost way. At best, it produces superficial, temporary results. At worst, it becomes a manipulative tool leaders and consulting firms use to manage resistance to change instead of creating true ownership and commitment.

Today, leaders are aware of two essential truths. First, command-and-control behavior does not work. Second, they cannot bring about necessary change alone. They must develop within the organization the necessary commitment to action so that strategic initiatives become reality. The best and the brightest minds can produce brilliant strategies, but without an agile, flexible, engaged organization that is willing to implement them, these strategies are useless. Successful strategy implementation requires people at all levels of the organization who care about the outcome, people who have the necessary ownership, commitment, and will to implement them. Without this level of engagement the most daring, ingenious plan becomes leadership's abandoned child, left on the doorstep to fend for itself in a dangerous world.

Despite this awareness, leaders must constantly fight the urge to control the outcome and to work solely with an inner circle of trusted colleagues as they face immense pressure from rapidly changing markets, enormous competitive forces, and technology that is changing so fast that yesterday's innovation is today's antique. The paradox is that in order for leaders to get what they want—an engaged organization that has the will and willingness to adapt to swiftly changing conditions—they must let go of the belief that they alone have the answer. Indeed, they must involve more people in the change process than they ever thought prudent or possible. In doing so, it is necessary for leaders to join with people from all levels and functions of the organization, along with other important stakeholders such as customers, suppliers, and even community members to create the future together.

However, current change management practices do not support this behavior; rather, they appeal to the leader's desire for certainty and control. Even the words *change management* appeal to a leader's desire to control the outcomes, as if change were something that could be predicted and controlled from beginning to end. The current change management paradigm, which I describe fully in Chapter One, is a refined attempt to increase participation and involvement in the change process while at the same time assuring predictability and control. It is better than anything that preceded it, yet it has already succumbed to bureaucratic pressures and the need to control the outcomes.

At this point you might be thinking, *Wait a minute here, I have a business to run. All this stuff about involving more people and generating commitment sounds good, but it requires too much time and energy. Besides, who's going to keep things running while we're off contemplating our navels? There are products to be made, orders to be shipped, and customers who expect us to be there and do our job. And, even if I did these things, who else would care about the whole organization the way I do?*

For those of you who say the cost of engagement is too high, I would like to reflect on comments that my colleagues and I hear all too frequently in organizations. It is not uncommon for people to say, "We always have time to fix things but we never have time to do it right the first time." The same is true for organizational change. You can either take the time to invest in engaging the organization from the very beginning of your change process, or you can pay the exorbitant price of convincing a fearful, distrusting organization that what you have created for it is in everyone's best interest and will actually work. For those who say the cost of engagement is too high, I ask, what is the price of disengagement?

Terms of Engagement: Changing the Way We Change Organizations is the first book to challenge the widely accepted change management paradigm. It provides leaders at all levels of the organization—all those who initiate, design, and implement change—with a set of principles for bringing about change in a turbulent world. It is not a methodology, nor is it a set of techniques; rather, it is a set of principles that everyone can fall back on when faced with new and different situations. Whether you are working in an organization of five or twenty-five thousand, the principles of *Terms of Engagement* will enable you to design your own techniques and methods for change to fit your unique circumstances.

One of my colleagues, Julie Beedon, recalls the benefits of working from a set of principles when solving problems: "My mathematics teacher at school always told me to go back to the first principles. When I was struggling to make sense of a confusing mathematical mess, that advice always paid off. Familiarity with those principles enabled me to tackle the most unusual questions, designed by examiners to throw you into panic, with confidence and resilience." Similarly, familiarity with the principles in this book will provide you with flexibility to meet the changing needs of your organization and the specific environment in which it operates. When you understand principles, unusual situations are not a cause for panic. Rather, you can approach them with confidence, secure in the knowledge that, by staying with the principles, you will create new responses that fit the unique circumstances that confront you. Throughout this book, there are numerous examples, how-tos, and case histories. They are here to serve as examples of the application of these principles and to stimulate your thinking by showing you what is possible; they are not meant to be the last word.

The principles described in *Terms of Engagement* will help you to engage people in dramatic organizational change. They will not teach you how to manipulate people so that they *feel* engaged, but rather how to create environments where true engagement is possible. Thus they will provide you with a strategy for creating a new organization that can be successful in today's world. These are the four principles:

- Widening the circle of involvement
- Connecting people to each other and ideas
- Creating communities for action
- Embracing democracy

These principles form an integrated set whose maximum benefit is achieved only when all four are applied simultaneously. Leaders who successfully apply these deceptively simple yet extremely ambitious principles reap the benefits of creating organizations that are able to respond effectively to the chaos, confusion, and complexity of an ever-changing business environment. In these organizations

- People grasp the big picture, fully understanding the dangers and opportunities.
- There is urgency and energy as people become aligned around a common purpose and create new directions.
- Accountability is fully distributed throughout the organization as people come to understand the whole system.
- Collaboration across organizational boundaries increases because people are connected to the issues and to each other.
- Broad participation quickly identifies performance gaps and their solutions, improving productivity and customer satisfaction.
- Creativity is sparked when people from all levels and functions, along with customers, suppliers, and important others, contribute their best ideas.
- Capacity for future changes increases as people develop the skills and processes to meet not just the current challenges but future challenges as well.

Structure of the Book

Terms of Engagement consists of three parts. In Part One, "The Problem and the Solution," I identify the problems with the current change management paradigm in Chapter One, "Why Change Management Needs Changing." A powerful alternative to current practice is then presented in Chapter Two, "The Engagement Paradigm."

Part Two, "Producing the Engaged Organization," explores the four principles for producing an engaged organization. In this section, each principle is discussed in a separate chapter that includes how-tos for implementation.

Part Three, "Getting Started," begins with a chapter titled "When Engagement Disengages: Some Words of Caution Before You Begin." The engagement paradigm is not a panacea and not immune to abuse and misuse. This is the "buyer beware" chapter of the book, in which I alert the reader to the minefields on the road to engagement. The final chapter, "The Power of Engagement," identifies eight specific issues the engagement paradigm can help you tackle, including the introduction of new technology, the increase in mergers, acquisitions, and alliances, and growing dissociation from communities.

Your journey toward developing a flexible and powerful organization starts with the first chapter of *Terms of Engagement*. Why not begin now?

PART 1

The Problem and the Solution

1

Why Change Management Needs Changing

You sit bolt upright drenched in sweat. After fumbling for your glasses, you look at the clock radio. The green blur slowly comes into focus and to your disbelief you see that it's three in the morning. The fear that started out a few weeks ago as a rumble in your stomach now takes over your body in the form of full-blown terror. You now feel absolutely certain that the major change you are responsible for bringing to your organization is on the verge of collapse. You will not sleep again tonight.

How did it come to this? You were filled with hope, pride, and enthusiasm from the moment you were chosen to lead this effort. The recognition was long in coming, but the organization signified your worth with this assignment. You started out by gathering your best people together and informing them of the challenges that were ahead. It did not take long for them to share your enthusiasm. With this all-star team, success was all but certain. Next, you hired the best consultants. Their promise was seductive: not only would they provide you with the latest answers and most up-to-date techniques, their change management specialists would show you how to manage any resistance. And sure enough, your consultants and all-star team together produced creative solutions—innovative strategies and plans to move the organization forward. Yet now, as you lie here staring at the ceiling, a loud voice inside you says, "The organization isn't supporting this. The resisters will win out." All the late nights and hard work have been for naught. The minutes seem like hours as you try to figure out what to do next. The questions and recriminations come rapidly. You wonder where you went wrong. And is there anything you can do now to turn things around? You have few—if any—answers.

If you've found yourself in this situation, you've probably been following the conventional wisdom for creating organizational change. You hired a reputable consulting firm, which brought in knowledgeable people who provided important information. And because everyone knew this change would be difficult, you also brought in change management consultants to ease the way. To ensure buy-in, they formed steering committees and design groups representing all levels and departments. Buy-in would occur because there was input from all levels and functions and people would feel that they were represented in the process. Participants in these groups worked long hours, were committed to the task, and were genuinely excited about the challenge of bringing about this important change. Yet the rest of the organization viewed those working on the project with suspicion and distrust, wondering what "they" were going to do to "us." This prevailing attitude of fear, along with its accompanying confusion, is now threatening to bring the change process to its knees.

Who is to blame in such a situation? The leaders? The consultants? The employees who put in so many long hours in the various committees? Are they all incompetent?

Actually, no one is to blame. Everyone followed current best practice. The change management paradigm that guided their actions is widely accepted as the way to bring about organizational change. As I mentioned in the Introduction, the problem is that these practices—once considered leading-edge—are no longer sufficient in today's business climate. Though well-intentioned, these efforts to bring about acceptance for essential change often have the opposite effect: they alienate the very people whose support is essential to success.

In the name of participation, the current change management paradigm actually increases bureaucracy, reinforces top-down management, and increases cynicism and resistance, thereby making change more difficult than it needs to be.

The Change Management Paradigm

First a little history. The issue of how leaders bring about change has been with us since human beings first began to work together. Consider for a moment the problems Moses encountered as he attempted to convince a reluctant band of Israelites to leave Egypt—their initial rejection of the Ten Commandments and their trials and tribulations in the desert. And finally, at the moment they were about to enter into the promised land, God did not consider Moses himself a suitable leader to make that journey. Leadership is a thankless job.

The Western archetype of leadership is that of a hero or heroine who somehow convinces the reluctant multitudes that change is necessary. Whether it be a king or queen from the Middle Ages, a president, a war hero, John Wayne, Moses, or the bold CEO who leads a corporate turnaround, the story is the same. The heroic figure, because of insight, charisma, and leadership skills, is able to convince a reluctant group of people to do something they might otherwise not want to do. This archetype reached its zenith during World War II when the world seemed full of heroic leaders. Some who dominated the world scene were Winston Churchill, Charles de Gaulle, Dwight D. Eisenhower, Douglas MacArthur, Franklin Roosevelt, and Harry Truman. Today this leadership ideal is very much alive. I am calling the type of change based on this archetype *leader-driven change.*

Heroic leaders have always surrounded themselves with advisers. However, as society and organizations became more complex, experts with specialized knowledge were required to produce needed changes. Leaders now sought advice beyond the boundaries of their own organization. Advisers were outsourced. Soon large consulting firms with legions of consultants made their debut on the scene. These firms brought industrial engineering, strategic planning, reengineering, and killer apps to organizations that desperately needed these critical technologies. Eventually, these consulting firms became so powerful that leaders turned over the whole change process to them. The heroic leader now serves as a cheerleader for change processes developed and led by experts. I call this type of change *process-driven change.*

Meanwhile a third type of change process, which I call *team-driven change,* was developing. While leader- and process-driven change largely ignored employees, team-driven change processes recognized two important facts: First, employees at all levels can make enormous contributions toward improving organizations. Second, without the support and commitment of employees at all levels significant organizational change is impossible. Examples of team-driven change include quality circles, employee involvement processes, and team-based organizations. Here we also find the heroic leader as a cheerleader for the process, in the worst cases abdicating responsibility in the name of employee participation and in the best cases becoming one of the many, a leader with a voice but not the only one whose voice counts.

Early efforts at team-driven change were implemented through a significant innovation called the *parallel organization,* the first mechanism to materially involve employees at all levels of the organization in the change process. It was like giving water to someone dying of thirst. In part, its success can be attributed to the depth of deprivation present in organizations at the time it was introduced. As water brings life to a dehydrated person, employee involvement processes brought new energy, innovation, and vigor to dying organizations. For the first time, a worker on an auto assembly line had the power not only to stop the line at once upon noticing a problem but also to work with coworkers to identify solutions and recommend courses of action.

Because of the success of team-driven change, it began to be noticed by those specializing in process-driven change. They recognized how the parallel organization was able to increase ownership and commitment to the change process. Since the lack of employee commitment and support is a serious problem in process-driven change, they began to wonder if the solution could be found within team-driven change. What would happen if the structure for bringing about team-driven change, the parallel organization, was integrated with process-driven change? The benefits of expert consulting associated with process-driven change would be combined with the increased employee ownership and commitment that occurs in team-driven change. From this union, change management was born. Its promise was to integrate the benefits of both processes, promoting the creativity, ownership, and commitment that occurs through participation while providing the alleged business focus of process-driven change. By 1990 this integration of the parallel organization with process-driven change had become the standard process for implementing organizational change. Ten years later, it is still entrenched: there is hardly an organizational change process, from changing organizational cultures to developing new information systems, that does not have a parallel organization, and its accompanying change management paradigm, at its core. As in process-driven and team-driven change the heroic leader in the change management paradigm is relegated to cheerleading the effort. Table 1-1 summarizes the key features of the four approaches to organizational change.

Change management was a significant leap forward and a noble attempt to improve the way we change organizations. However, change management has both structural and cultural flaws that produce the significant negative consequences for organizations that I mentioned earlier in this chapter: increased cynicism, resistance, and bureaucracy, and reinforcement of top-down management—in other words, the Dilbert organization. To see why this significant innovation failed to fulfill its promise and ultimately lost its way, take a few minutes to examine the fundamental structure behind change management, the parallel organization.

Table 1-1 Historical Approaches to Change

	Leader-Driven	Process-Driven	Team-Driven	Change Management
Form	• Leader produces change	• Experts produce change	• Teams produce change	• Experts and teams produce change
Examples	• Command and control leadership style	• Industrial engineering • Strategic planning • Information technology	• Quality circles and employee involvement • Team-based organizations	• Reengineering • Supply chain improvement
Change Strategy	• Leader meets with advisers and announces change • Leader uses personal power to bring about change	• Experts identify and recommend required changes • Experts lead change process • Leaders lend their power to experts	• Employees identify and recommend needed changes • Leaders approve • Parallel organization	• Experts initiate and lead change with employee input • Leaders approve • Parallel organization
Values	• Leaders know best	• Consultants know best	• Teams know best	• Consultants with input from teams know best
Why It Worked	• Leaders have the most knowledge and power • Uneducated workforce • Fits values of larger culture	• Consultants have specialized knowledge • Leaders lend power to consultants • Uneducated workforce	• Those closest to the work have the most knowledge about how to fix day-to-day problems • Powerless employees given a say • Educated workforce	• Provided a business focus to team-driven change • Brought new levels of commitment and ownership to process-driven change • Educated workforce

Why It No Longer Works				
	• Increasing availability of information, a highly educated workforce, and rising democracy makes the few deciding for the many no longer acceptable	• Increasing availability of information, a highly educated workforce, and rising democracy makes the few deciding for the many no longer acceptable	• Increasing availability of information, a highly educated workforce, and rising democracy makes the few deciding for the many no longer acceptable	• Increasing availability of information, a highly educated workforce, and rising democracy makes the few deciding for the many no longer acceptable
	• Addressing complex problems in a rapidly changing environment requires more knowledge and input than are possessed by a single leader	• Addressing complex problems in a rapidly changing environment requires more knowledge and input than are possessed by a leader and his or her consultant	• Addressing complex problems in a rapidly changing environment requires more knowledge and input than are possessed by employees alone	• Addressing complex problems in a rapidly changing environment requires more knowledge and input than are possessed by consultants and a select few employees
	• Rapid implementation requires a critical mass of people at all levels who are connected to the outcomes—not just the leader	• Rapid implementation requires a critical mass of people at all levels who are committed to the outcomes—not just the consultants and those employees they have asked for input	• Rapid implementation requires a critical mass of people at all levels who are committed to the outcomes—not just lower-level employees	• Rapid implementation requires a critical mass of people at all levels who are committed to the outcomes—not a select few, not just consultants, not just leaders, but everyone

How the Parallel Organization Works

The parallel organization is made up of a series of teams or groups with interlocking memberships. Typically, a change effort is composed of a sponsor group, a steering committee, and one or more design groups. The sponsor group is a cross-functional team of senior leaders who lend their support to the needed changes. Their role is to initiate the process, cheerlead the effort, and provide funding. They are not involved in the day-to-day development of the change process, but their approval is usually required for key results. The steering committee is composed of people representing a cross-section of the organization from all levels and functions (including union leadership in unionized settings). Their role is the day-to-day management of the change process. Design groups are also cross-functional and multilevel. Their role is to develop the specifics of the change, developing new organizational structures or redesigning core processes as needed.

These three groups—sponsor team, steering team, and design team—make up the parallel organization, which operates alongside the regular organization to manage and accelerate the change process (see Figure 1-1). This streamlined organization, because of its reduced organizational levels and cross-functional membership, is designed to eliminate the barriers to change that exist within the regular organization. The parallel organization, then, is the platform for bringing about needed change.

Figure 1-1 The Parallel Organization

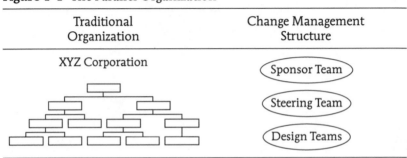

What the Parallel Organization Claims to Do

The parallel organization is based on the following assumptions:

Diverse membership in the teams, with key decision makers in the room, provides a vehicle for overcoming organizational red tape and is the most efficient governance structure for the change process. The three levels—sponsors, steering committee, and design groups—collapse the regular organization's seven or eight levels. This reduction in levels, combined with the cross-functional nature of the teams, puts all key decision makers in the room. New proposals—instead of having to wend their way through the current bureaucracy—can be adopted quickly within the parallel organization's structure.

High-quality solutions are assured by populating the teams with the "best and the brightest" from the organization. Other members of the organization will feel that these groups represent their interests.

The parallel organization breaks down organizational silos while creating high-quality solutions. Cross-functional and multilevel membership guarantees solutions that favor the total organization or system rather than a particular unit or function.

Cooperative team behaviors learned by the team members will be transmitted throughout the organization. In other words, the parallel organization will act as a vehicle for learning to work in a participative, flatter organizational structure. Committee members learn participatory behaviors and group decision-making skills that are not dependent on authority or position. The belief is that members will then transfer their new knowledge into the day-to-day workings of the regular organization.

Consensus decision making by the committees will assure both high-quality solutions and buy-in of key organization members. Fundamental to the concept of the parallel organization is the belief that the change process is best managed by a select few; that is, the members of the sponsor team, steering committee, and design team or teams. Their job, along with the consultants who support them, is to identify needed changes, develop solutions, and then create buy-in for the process.

Ensuring organizational acceptance of needed changes is an important purported benefit of the parallel organization. The thinking goes like this: First, the cross-functional and cross-hierarchical nature of the teams will cause organization members to believe they were represented in the process. Second, because the teams are made up of people who have high credibility within the organization, the rest of the organization will readily accept their ideas. Finally, as a result of their positive experiences in the parallel organization, team members will champion the process throughout the organization and be able to convince others of the value of the proposed changes.

Why the Change Management Paradigm Does Not Work

Although revolutionary at its inception, the change management paradigm is no longer sufficient for today's workforce and rapidly changing work environment. While it can claim some positive features, such as including more people in process-driven change, it also produces the unintended negative consequences mentioned earlier: increased cynicism, resistance, and bureaucracy, and reinforcement of top-down management.

As devastating as these consequences are, they are merely symptoms of larger factors, whose root causes can be found in the process itself and its misuse as it became mainstream. Together these six factors account for the ineffectiveness of change management:

▪ Allowing the few to decide for the many
▪ Isolating leaders and organization members from one another
▪ Separating the design process from the implementation process
▪ Adopting the parallel organization but not its underlying values
▪ Making process improvements primary and cultural shifts secondary
▪ Incongruency in the process itself

Allowing the Few to Decide for the Many

The current change management paradigm, with its reliance on the few developing solutions for the many, guarantees that the implementation process will be more difficult than it needs to be. People develop a negative bias toward change when they do not feel their voices are being heard. Minimal information about the proposed changes causes the rumor mill to operate overtime and catastrophic scenarios to fill the hallways. In *Leading Change*, John Kotter says that most organizations undercommunicate about change by a factor of ten. This combination of minimal involvement in the change process and poor communication between the parallel organization and organization members guarantees that the crucial support needed for successful implementation will be withheld.

A parallel organization of even a hundred people is quite small in an organization employing thousands. The basic premise is that these select few, the best and the brightest, will develop the necessary organizational changes and then sell them to the many. But it is only after the solution is developed that any attempts at widespread involvement are made. After being excluded from the process of determining what the changes will be, people are given the so-called opportunity to decide how the new changes will be implemented. This typically does not feel like an opportunity at all, but more like a manipulation. Is it any wonder that this process increases resistance rather than reducing it?

The emphasis on picking the "best and the brightest" for the various committees leads many to believe that management is stacking the deck with people who will readily agree with its predetermined answer. Because organization members do not feel that their voices count, they quickly become cynical. Even when committees make efforts to conduct interviews to obtain employee thoughts and opinions, participants in the interview process often are distrustful of what the committee will do with their input. Did they really listen? Did they really understand, or are they just going to use the data selectively to reinforce previously held opinions? Because most teams do not do a good job of staying in contact with interview participants and providing feedback about how their data is used in developing the ultimate recommendations, the cynical view prevails.

Cynicism also increases because most design groups do not interview everyone. So people who are not part of the parallel organization and are not selected for an interview come to believe that they are really unimportant.

Isolating Leaders and Organization
Members from One Another

The committee structure of the parallel organization isolates leaders and organization members from one another. Instead of working together to bring their combined knowledge to bear on an issue, these groups work separately on their own discrete parts. Additionally, even though the parallel organization is an attempt to reduce organizational levels and red tape, its very structure of sponsor group, steering committee, and design teams indicates to all that the hierarchy, with its accompanying top-down management style, is very much intact.

I remember explaining the parallel organization concept to the vice president of a manufacturing organization. After hearing the virtues of this approach, the VP leaned back in his chair, thought about it for a few moments, and then said, "All you are doing here is creating another level of management with these committees!" Since he was a very authoritarian manager, I quickly labeled him as resistant and dismissed his insight. In retrospect, I see that he was correct. Over time, the committees of the parallel organization became another layer of management, isolating themselves from the workforce and adopting the authoritarian behaviors of the leadership when dealing with the organization. After a while, they even began to sound like management, complaining about people who don't get it and resisters who are getting in the way of progress. All of this in the name of participation.

Here is a scenario that I have witnessed repeatedly that demonstrates the problems of isolating leaders and organization members from each other. The design teams work feverishly to develop a set of proposals. They then spend as much time preparing for their presentation to the steering committee as they did developing their proposals because they know how important it is to present things well. At the steering committee meeting, the committee members put design team members on the hot seat. Soon everyone becomes defensive. Steering committee members feel that they are raising legitimate concerns while design team members start to believe that the steering committee has already determined the answer they want. The design team goes back and tries to give the steering committee what they want while staying true to their own beliefs. The steering committee waits for the next report, not quite understanding why the design team members are so defensive. After a number of iterations of this process, a decision is developed that the steering committee can support. Then the process repeats itself when the steering committee members review the proposed changes with the sponsor group.

Finally, relegating leaders to the role of cheerleaders is a significant flaw. In this role, leaders are often prevented from contributing valuable knowledge, expertise, and insights to the design teams that make up the parallel organization as proposals and plans are being developed. The only time they can contribute is when plans are brought to them for approval. So it's no surprise that when they do this, they are often seen as "raining on the parade" of the hardworking design teams and committee members. Leaders must be more than cheerleaders, they must be part and parcel of the change process.

Separating Planning from Doing

The inability to develop critical support for necessary changes can be traced back to the decision to separate the planning process from the implementation process. Separating change development from implementation is a critical mistake.

I often conduct the following exercise as part of management development programs. In the exercise, participants are divided into two teams. The first team is called the *planners* and the second team is called the *doers*. The planners are charged with developing a plan for how the doers are to put together a puzzle. The doers are supposed to execute the plan. Typically, the doers are sent out in the hall while the planners develop their plan. While in the hall, the doers usually develop negative feelings toward the planners. Sometimes they even use this time to figure out how to sabotage the work of the planners. Once the plan is developed, the planners summon the doers and give them instructions. When the two groups operate in the previously described fashion, they rarely complete the exercise within the prescribed one-hour time frame. But occasionally, the planners invite the doers into their deliberations and they both develop and execute the plan together. When this occurs, the task is usually completed within fifteen minutes. The current change management paradigm is behind the scenes in the first scenario: it involves relatively few people in the development of the plans for change, and then shifts its emphasis to involvement and buy-in only after important decisions have been made.

Adopting the Parallel Organization Without Its Underlying Values

A critical oversight occurred when the parallel organization became part of process-driven change. The structure was adopted without its accompanying values. This is a classic example of employing a technique without understanding or following its underlying principles. Because the parallel organization was seen as successful in bringing about change in some well-known organizations, many others tried to copy their success. However, they failed to adopt the principles of high employee involvement and participative decision making that were the cornerstone of the process. In the end, this failure has led to the ultimate misuse of the parallel organization and the change management paradigm itself.

As the parallel organization became more mainstream, the teams within the structure began to be consultant-led, rather than consultant-facilitated. The purpose of the teams within the parallel structure then shifted from leading the change process to being information resources to consultants and organization leaders. This was a shift away from empowerment.

Reengineering is a case in point. Although many reengineering consultants advocated the creation of a team-based organization, they believed that this could occur only after the organization was streamlined and downsized by the best and the brightest who populated the parallel organization. After the carnage, they fully expected a group of distrusting, traumatized survivors to come together and operate effectively in a cooperative environment. In the November 26, 1996, *Wall Street Journal,* Michael Hammer explains the failure of many reengineering projects. He points out that he forgot people. "I wasn't smart enough about that," he says. "I was reflecting my engineering background and was insufficiently appreciative of the human dimension. I've learned that's critical."

Concentrating on Process Improvements

As the parallel organization was adopted by process-driven change, the concept of shifting the organization's culture began to fade into the background and eventually disappeared entirely. What became primary was implementing the change, often through technology. Even though the development of new systems and structures required people to change the way they worked and the partners they worked with, these cultural aspects were deemed secondary. There are many examples of reorganizations and reengineering processes designed to create new internal working relationships or to improve customer service that completely ignored the cultural aspects of the change. People soon found themselves in new organizational configurations designed to produce cooperation, teamwork, and improved customer service while the old hierarchical silo culture remained unchanged. This failure to deal with the cultural aspects of change undermined the benefits of the system.

Consider a telephone company's recent experience. The committees of the parallel organization had created a brilliant design for a new organization aligned with the customer base, in which the previous organizational silos were replaced with integrated business units. Both the sponsors and the committee members believed that they had created a breakthrough for this stodgy old organization.

Yet the organization became paralyzed. Why? For over a year, the design group had made decisions behind closed doors. Although it actively solicited opinions, not all departments and levels of people felt included in the process. When it came time to roll out the new organization, there had been so many rumors that people were negatively disposed toward it.

In addition, there was little preparation for working in this new team-based, customer-focused environment. Most people brought their old hierarchical, silo-based mentality into the new structure—with predictable results. Warnings by the leadership that the wolves were at the door and that the organization could be out of business if needed changes did not occur were met with apathy. In response, managers labeled those who were not cheerleaders for the new organization as obstructionists. Before long, they were reduced to demanding that employees either support the new organization or choose other employment. In the end, the promise of the reengineered organization—greater responsiveness to customers and increased collaboration and teamwork—was never realized. Leadership inadvertently created resistance by ignoring the cultural aspects of the change and focusing solely on reengineering the organization.

Fostering Incongruency

The change management paradigm soon developed its own incongruency. In practice, the words and the music simply do not match. While the goals of many change management processes remain to improve process and systems, to make work easier, to reduce organizational bureaucracy, and to improve teamwork and cooperation, these changes are too often introduced in an authoritarian fashion. This creates a disconnect between the espoused goals of the change process and how the change process is conducted. In *Overcoming Organizational Defenses,* Chris Argyris states that when this disparity exists, people experience the change process as a fad, and organizational defensiveness and resistance increase.

Additionally, the emphasis on involving people only to provide input to leaders and consultants so that they can make the necessary decisions leaves people with a half-empty feeling. They appreciate being asked, but would much rather have a say in making the final decisions. Similarly, the emphasis on involving people only when it comes time for implementation also leaves people feeling lukewarm. Some input is better than none, but it is not sufficient.

It is a sad irony that the experience of many change management consultants in major consulting firms often mirrors that of their clients. Neither group is brought into the change process early enough to make a significant contribution, and both groups wind up feeling not valued. In these firms, change management is usually the stepchild of other practices, the real rainmakers of the firm, and change management tends to be viewed as the practice that gets the client's employees to go along with the changes that the firm advocates. The goal, once again, is to reduce resistance rather than develop true ownership and commitment. Rarely are the firms' change management consultants brought into the consultation at the very beginning, when true involvement and participation can occur. Rather, in a similar manner to their clients, they are brought in during the implementation process, after all the major decisions have been made.

Finally, the change management paradigm assumes that people will resist change. In fact, the phrase *change management* is often seen as code for a process to manage the inevitable resistance. Because it assumes that people will be predisposed to resist the new, it treats them as objects that must be won over rather than people who would be willing partners in creating a new and better organization. It limits their participation rather than supporting it. It minimizes rather than maximizes information flow. Imagine how your change process would be different if you treated people as willing partners as opposed to resisters who must be converted.

Some Telling Examples of Change Management Today

The two stories in this section provide examples of the current change management paradigm and how the engagement paradigm provides a powerful alternative. Detroit Edison began the change process using the change management paradigm but found that it made life very difficult. By contrast, Timberland used the engagement paradigm successfully to bring about needed change within the marketing organization.

The Detroit Edison Story

For over a year, Detroit Edison managers had been working to improve their supply-chain process. They were following the traditional change management paradigm complete with a sponsoring group, a steering committee, and a set of commodity teams, along with an army of expert consultants. Despite the hard work of many people from inside and outside the organization, they had little to show for it. The sponsors were frustrated by the lack of progress, the steering committee shared this frustration, and the commodity teams . . . well, they just could not understand why they could not get the organization to support the changes they were proposing. In spite of its critical importance to the organization, most people greeted the supply-chain improvement process with yawns. The only ones who seemed to care were members of the various committees—and even they were starting to show signs of disillusionment. Fortunately, this story has a successful conclusion. The next installment—in Chapter Two—describes how Detroit Edison abandoned the change management approach to supply-chain improvement in favor of the engagement paradigm with dramatic results.

The Timberland Story

When Lisa MacPherson, vice president of marketing for Timberland (an outdoor boot and apparel company), recognized the need to shift the marketing organization's culture, she decided to take a new approach. Instead of creating endless committees to deal with needed changes, she engaged the entire marketing force in creating a new, vibrant marketing organization. The results were remarkable. In a large group session that lasted three days, all sixty-five marketing employees learned about the marketing organization's history, discovered how work flowed through their organization, identified key disconnects in their process, and created both a long-term vision and some concrete first steps.

A new spirit of cooperation and enthusiasm was born within marketing that was noticed even by those outside of marketing who did not attend the session. Cross-functional groups sprung up to address long-standing problems. People and departments engaged with each other, moving from a silo orientation to one of cooperation. Because everyone understood how what they did affected others, organization members were able to identify and remove roadblocks. For example, advertising agencies traditionally were dealt with one at a time, causing much confusion and duplication. Now all the advertising agencies that work with Timberland joined them in a large meeting and a coordinated set of actions were developed. Another example: As a result of the first off-site meeting, two department members on their own created a new marketing organizational structure to remove some of the roadblocks that were identified during the session. At a subsequent large group session, they presented their ideas to the marketing organization, got feedback, and modified their proposal. This was then adopted by the marketing organization. As a result of efforts like these, within a few short weeks, a new sense of purpose, friendliness, energy, and congeniality spread over the department.

Recently I spoke with Lisa about her experience. Here is what we said:

RHA: Why did you want to involve the whole marketing organization?

LMP: What I recognized immediately was the need for changes in both our processes and culture. I did not want to take the time for traditional waterfall approaches to change. I wanted everyone in the organization to understand the need for change and have the same imperatives. I was afraid that a top-down approach with many committees would dilute the message.

Over the years, I have recognized that organizational task forces produce a great deal of energy for task force members but not for the rest of the organization. I wanted everyone in the organization to have the same level of passion that I had seen within task forces. My gut instinct was that, in order for us to succeed, we needed to engage everyone.

RHA: What was most difficult for you during this process?

LMP: I had to let go of the desire to fix or control things when I thought the outcome would be different from mine. I had to trust the fact that if we provided enough information, people would create good solutions—although those solutions might be different from mine.

Deep down inside I was afraid. What if I brought all these people together and we just stared at each other? Worse yet, what if my assessment of the organization was wrong? What if people did not see the problems I saw? What would I do then?

RHA: Were any of these fears realized?

LMP: No. In fact, it was just the opposite. Within the first few minutes of our large group session, I knew it would work. People were excited to be there. They spoke honestly with each other and confirmed the breakdowns we were all experiencing. Not only did people develop a greater understanding of how we function as an organization, they also understood the whole marketing process from the inside out.

RHA: What advice do you have for others?

LMP: Trust your gut. If you think you need to do this, you probably do. Don't let the skeptics and naysayers dissuade you. Trust the process—your people will step up to this. Our planning team was invaluable, more so than I would have predicted. Be as involved as you expect your people to be; ask of yourself the same level of participation that you expect from others. Do not abdicate your responsibilities as a leader.

Summary

The twenty-year-old change management paradigm needs changing. This once-innovative approach no longer meets the needs of organizations in today's complex and rapidly changing environment. Flawed in both concept and use, it produces cynicism and resistance instead of an engaged organization. In the next chapter, I will lay out the basics of a new standard for change, the engagement paradigm.

2

The Engagement Paradigm

The old change management paradigm, with its requisite committees, teams, and heavy consultant influence, contains the seeds
of its own destruction. As promised in the first chapter, here is
how Detroit Edison dealt with the problems it was having with its
supply-chain improvement process.

Detroit Edison Continued

When the leaders of Detroit Edison recognized that the process was
in danger of collapsing, they decided that drastic action was required.
They proceeded to redesign the supply-chain improvement process
using the principles of the engagement paradigm. Switching processes in midstream was not an easy task: they did not want to throw

out the good analytical work that had been done, yet they needed to signal a shift in direction. The issues they faced were how to involve more people in the process so as to build greater commitment and how to build on the previous work while moving in a new direction. Using the engagement paradigm, in a few short months, they engaged over nine hundred people—one-third of the organization—in the supply-chain process in a series of large group sessions attended by employees at all levels, customers, suppliers, contractors, and key union officials. To avoid the "flavor of the month" problem that could have occurred as a result of shifting the paradigms, they first developed a communication and education strategy to explain the change in direction. Second, they used the work to date on the supply-chain process as their starting point, carefully creating links from the previous work to the present. And when it came to implementing the new process, they used current projects that required supply-chain emphasis. This had the effect of grounding the supply-chain improvement process in real work, not imposing something extra on an overburdened organization.

Today there are over twenty-six active supply-chain improvement projects at Detroit Edison, with savings in the millions and growing. Engagement at all levels of the organization has replaced withdrawal and lack of interest. Furthermore, when the nuclear division needed to create a vision and strategy to meet the challenges of deregulation, it too used the engagement paradigm. Division management involved more than 650 people (over half of the organization) in a three-day conference that set the direction for meeting the challenges of a new deregulated marketplace and at the same time created a critical mass of connected people who are committed to making that vision a reality.

Hewlett-Packard

"We were like a refugee camp. We worked for the same company but spoke different languages. Shock resulting from a downturn in our industry permeated everyone. We were confused and without organizational homes. Survival meant creating a new way of life," explains Mike Freeman, former director of Hewlett-Packard's Micro-Electronics Operation. "The challenges were enormous. We had five different organizations, we were located on one site, and we had to transform ourselves into an integrated manufacturing organization in the face of a changing and uncertain market."

Mike and his leadership team instinctively recognized that successfully producing the required changes meant fully engaging the workforce. They recognized that the current change management paradigm was too slow and would not create the deep levels of commitment, collaboration, and capacity necessary for future changes. To redesign their organization, they held five large group sessions that involved nearly everyone in the process. They successfully engaged the organization, converting this refugee camp into an efficient, collaborative, customer-focused organization, one that has recorded productivity improvements of 18 percent each year for the last five years.

How did Mike and his people do it? Like Detroit Edison, they transformed the entire organization by using the engagement paradigm.

Mike and his leadership team employed two innovative concepts to ensure that the change process was not perceived as another management fad. The first was the *throttle* concept. Increasing the throttle during slack times and pulling back on the throttle during times of stress gave the organization the necessary breathing space to develop and incorporate crucial changes, and allowed the leaders to manage the amount of change taking place within the organization at any one time. Instead of constantly piling one change initiative after another on top of the organization until it collapsed, they actually made decisions to start and stop different change initiatives. They judged the organization's capacity to handle change and acted accordingly. This is almost unheard of today, when organizations are under a constant barrage of change initiatives. Second, they wanted to make sure that as leaders they were not acting incongruently, so they developed the *coach* concept. Outside consultants were brought in to observe the team's leadership behavior and provide feedback. The goal was to make sure they were leading in a way that was consistent with the engagement paradigm and that supported the espoused goals of the change process. The leadership team's decision to use coaches was a stroke of genius. By opening themselves up to scrutiny from others, they demonstrated that they were not above the change process. Further, they realized that success required increased levels of collaboration and teamwork from everyone in the organization, and that they had to lead the way. By using coaches, the leadership team showed that this change process was for everyone.

When organizations use the engagement paradigm, they do more than simply manage change. The engagement paradigm produces collaboration across boundaries, increases teamwork, creates partnerships with customers and suppliers, and builds organizations that have the capacity to respond to tomorrow's challenges.

A New Paradigm

Ask business leaders why their recent change effort did not live up to its promise and they invariably answer not that they got the strategy wrong, but that they were unable to develop sufficient organizational support for the needed changes. What they often fail to recognize is that *the very change management process they employed is the root cause of the problem.* Rather than engaging the organization in critical change, the current change management paradigm disengages the very people whose support is essential to success. Unfortunately, many leaders, failing to recognize that the paradigm they are using is the problem, redouble their efforts to make it work, resulting in increased frustration on their part and increased alienation on the part of the employees. It is no accident that Scott Adams has become the voice of the disengaged. His Dilbert cartoons symbolize the frustration of people who do not believe that their voices count.

Today, leaders are under tremendous pressure from markets, customers, and competition to bring needed changes to their organization. These leaders do not intentionally go about creating more material for Dilbert. They desperately want to engage people in the issues that are vital to the organization's success. They want willing partners. They want people who are engaged rather than cynical, people who are ready to put their wholehearted selves into bringing about the required changes rather than people who sit on the sidelines and take the attitude that "this too shall pass."

Ask anyone who has participated on steering committees or design groups about their experience, and they will respond by saying, "Wouldn't it be great if everyone could have the experience we had? Wouldn't it be great if everyone could have learned what we learned?" In these responses is the key to moving beyond the change management paradigm. This involves the application of the four key principles mentioned in the introduction, which I'll describe briefly here to give you an overview. Chapters Three through Six provide a more detailed explanation of these principles along with examples of their application.

Widening the Circle of Involvement

Mere buy-in is no longer an acceptable goal. We must move toward deeply engaging people in the change process itself, creating a critical mass of energetic people who design and support necessary changes. *Widening the circle of involvement* means going beyond the dozens that are typically involved in current change practices and involving hundreds, even thousands of employees. In practical terms, widening the circle of involvement means expanding who gets to participate in a change process in two critical ways. The first is by including new and different voices. The second is by expanding the number of people in order to create a critical mass for change so that the few are no longer left in the position of deciding for the many. In addition to creating a critical mass for change, widening the circle of involvement also enhances innovation, adaptation, and learning.

Connecting People to Each Other

When people connect with each other and to powerful ideas, creativity and action are ensured. Barriers to the flow of information and new ideas are lowered as people forge links with others. Work also flows more smoothly, because people learn how what they do fits into the larger whole, and how to access needed resources.

When people connect with each other, they become known to each other. They stop being stereotypes, roles, functions and members of that hated "other." They become human beings with their own real-life issues and concerns. People who are doing the best they can to get the job done. People with unique talents to share. People with mortgages and families, who are trying to manage their lives. Connection begins with matching a name with a face, but it evolves to understanding who that person is, how they think, and what matters to them. Connection does not require sharing your deepest personal feelings; however, it does mean getting to know people beyond the facades of role and title.

Creating Communities for Action

Meeting today's challenges cannot be done by any one person single-handedly. We need a community of people who willingly provide their talents and insights to address increasingly complex issues. Community is important because one person no longer has *the* answer. Answers reside in all of us.

When we create community, we move beyond a group of people who may have personal connections with each other to developing a group of connected people who have both the will and willingness to work together to accomplish a goal that has meaning for them. Creating a sense of community in organizations is not easy because the requirements of mechanistic structures run contrary to what it takes to build community. Nevertheless, we cannot ignore this task.

Embracing Democracy

Democracy is the best form the human race has developed for people to come together, discuss and resolve issues, and act. It is through the democratic process that issues of self-interest versus the common good and minority versus majority opinion are dealt with in a way that ensures support and follow-through for the chosen course of action. Internationally today, there is more democracy, more freedom of information, and more freedom of expression than there has ever been. In this world, imposed change is no longer acceptable. Change grounded in democratic principles has the best chance for success.

Democratic principles provide an ethical foundation and a moral fiber for the change process in business as well as political life. They produce trust and confidence in both the change process and those who are leading it. They are universal principles that speak to the human spirit, the desire to be free, the desire to have a say, and the desire to shape one's own destiny.

The New Paradigm in Action

These key principles are the foundation of a new model for change I call the *engagement paradigm*. While building on the wisdom of the change management paradigm, the engagement paradigm provides a framework for developing not only the support but also the enthusiastic engagement of the entire organization. Here is what you can expect when you follow the four key principles:

- People grasp the issues, become aligned around a common purpose, and create new directions because they understand both the dangers and the opportunities.
- Urgency and energy are produced to create a new future.
- Free-flowing information and cooperation replace organizational silos because people are connected to the issues and to each other.
- Broad participation quickly identifies performance gaps and their solutions, improving productivity and customer satisfaction.
- Creativity is sparked when people from all levels and functions, along with customers, suppliers, and important others, contribute their best ideas.
- Capacity for future changes increases as people develop the skills and processes to meet not just the current challenges, but future challenges as well.

A Brief History of the Engagement Paradigm

The engagement paradigm is the result of over twenty-five years of consulting experience. Initially my colleagues and I believed deeply in the change management paradigm and struggled to make it work. We even had our share of successes. Nevertheless, we felt a nagging sense of unease, a quiet whisper deep inside that something was wrong with this approach. Our clients amplified the message by saying that the change management processes we were using were too slow, overly bureaucratic, and did not create the necessary ownership and buy-in to support effective change.

Initially we heard our clients' requests as a need to speed up the process. It was just taking too long. Organizations could no longer afford to spend twelve to eighteen months designing a change and then another year or more in implementation. The world would pass them by while they were off planning. So, being good consultants, we said the answer to the speed question was—add more consultants! In a limited sense we were right. By adding more consultants to the process, we were able to shorten the time it took to design needed changes. However, one critical problem remained: How to develop the necessary ownership and commitment that successful implementation requires. Reducing the design time solved only half the problem, because while the design process was going on, those not involved were becoming increasingly apprehensive about what "they" were creating for "us." Thus we inadvertently increased resistance to the change process rather than developing support.

We continued to try to improve the change management paradigm by adjusting its component parts, adding more consultants, making little changes here and there. However, we soon realized that mere tinkering was not sufficient. A radically new and different approach was needed. This approach had to involve more people sooner and with greater depth than anything we had ever done before. Ironically, our clients had been giving us the answer all along. As I noted earlier, members of parallel organizations often said, "Wouldn't it be great if everyone in the organization could have the experience we had?" Clearly, this was a request to move beyond the few to the many and involve the whole organization in the change process. My colleagues and I finally heard and understood what they were saying. Once we understood this request, the question became how to do it.

The Conference Model

We did not set out to develop the engagement paradigm. Our initial efforts focused on creating a high-involvement process for redesigning organizations that we called the *Conference Model.* The Conference Model consists of an integrated series of large and small group sessions that deal with the following topics:

- Creating a vision for the future
- Creating partnerships with customers and suppliers
- Analyzing organizational processes
- Designing new organizational structures and processes

In these highly participatory sessions, employees—along with other important stakeholders such as customers and suppliers—examine the organization's history and present circumstances, and then create a future together.

The Conference Model has two unique features. First, it consists of a series of connected *conferences* that are held every four to six weeks. This series of linked conferences creates organizational momentum and allows issues to be addressed at increasing levels of depth. *Walkthrus,* the second unique feature, are mini-conferences held for those organization members who could not attend the main conferences. In these mini-conferences, participants are informed of the results of the large group sessions and are invited to provide input into the change process. Thus they receive updates on what has happened to date, and their input is incorporated into the proceedings prior to the next session. Walkthrus are more than briefings; in fact, they have the look and feel of the large group sessions.

Together, the combination of integrated conferences and walkthrus turns the current change management paradigm on its head.

Instead of small groups determining what needs to be changed and then selling it to the rest of the organization, a critical mass of the organization comes together to identify the future. Small groups may be needed after a conference, but their role is to add detail to what has been decided in the conferences, not to determine the nature and direction of the change process.

The Conference Model has been used successfully to redesign organizations and processes in a variety of settings such as health care, education, manufacturing, and government. It has also been used to create new organizational cultures and to support mergers and acquisitions.

It is recognized as part of a group of interventions that have revolutionized the practice of organizational change. Some of these other interventions include the Future Search Conference (a process by which diverse groups discover common futures); Real Time Strategic Change (a process for aligning and creating collective futures while developing new strategies and directions); Whole Scale Change (a process for connecting an organization so that it has one brain and one heart), and Participative Design (a process for the design of effective organizations). When you look at these interventions through the lens of the engagement paradigm you see that they are all in alignment with the engagement paradigm's four core principles.

Our initial efforts with the Conference Model focused on getting the technique right: how to design large group sessions to do the work that was previously done by small committees and how to involve those not present at the large group sessions in the change process. For each organization we worked with, we would begin by identifying how many conferences were needed, the activities that would make up each conference, how to configure the walkthrus, and how everything would flow together. During this time, in other words, we focused exclusively on developing and refining the mechanics. It was only after we were sure that the process worked in a wide variety of settings that we were able to step back and look at what was going on. In retrospect, it is clear that the Conference Model is a robust example of the engagement paradigm in action.

Birth of the Engagement Paradigm

What my colleagues and I saw was that conferences and walkthrus consistently produced excitement, energy, and engagement with participants. We saw that participants not only supported the decisions made in the conferences but implemented them as well. Our curiosity was piqued. Why did the Conference Model work? To answer this question, I began to examine the assumptions and principles behind our techniques. However, rather than confine ourselves to our own process, I looked at the other large group processes along with other theoretical constructs such as systems theory, learning theory, and complexity theory. What I saw particularly with large group processes, including our own Conference Model, was that although each process claimed to be principle-based the principles were used to explain why that methodology worked. I began to realize that what was needed was a way of thinking about change that was independent of methodology and could be applied in a wide variety of settings and circumstances. It became increasingly clear to me that methodology-based approaches to change could not provide the necessary innovation and flexibility to meet the requirements of complex organizations in rapidly changing environments. Similar to the mathematics example in the Introduction, if organizations were limited to only knowing techniques for organizational change without having a core set of principles to guide them they would always be in the situation of using formula approaches to change rather than creating change processes that fit their unique circumstances.

My search was not an easy one. It started with long lists of principles—macro principles, micro principles, design principles, leadership principles. In fact there were just too many principles! No one could possibly remember all of them. What was needed was a set of simple yet profound principles that leaders at all levels of the organization could use to guide their actions. After much refinement the four underlying principles that produce an engaged organization emerged, and the engagement paradigm was born. Since 1996 we have been teaching the engagement paradigm in the Association for Quality and Participation's

School for Managing and Leading Change and in workshops around the world. The stories and vignettes contained in *Terms of Engagement* are examples of the engagement paradigm in action. In particular, the Timberland, Detroit Edison, Washington Alliance for Better Schools, Berkeley, and First Union stories represent organizations where the change process was designed using the four principles of the engagement paradigm. Because of my history and familiarity with the Conference Model many of the other stories and vignettes in *Terms of Engagement* come from experiences with the Conference Model and are included as examples of the principles in action. But what makes the engagement paradigm different from the current change management paradigm?

Five Myths of the Engagement Paradigm

When I discuss the engagement paradigm with potential users, they often raise a familiar set of objections, which I am calling myths. These are the myths that keep leaders holding on to the familiar change management paradigm and prevent them from moving toward the engagement paradigm:

■ Unless I keep a tight rein, I cannot control the outcomes (or, the engagement paradigm means that I must completely let go).
■ We must keep a firewall between the organization and its stakeholders.
■ Productivity will suffer if I involve a lot of people.
■ The majority cannot be trusted to put the organization's interests first. Self-interest will take over.
■ Changes designed by the best and the brightest are cost-effective.

The first myth is that using the engagement paradigm requires leaders to let go completely. As leaders contemplate widening the circle of involvement and embracing democratic principles, they sometimes believe that these principles will require them to completely abdicate their legitimate authority, responsibility, and the ability to provide input based on their knowledge and experience. Nothing could be further from the truth. Widening the circle of involvement does not mean excluding leaders. In fact, their involvement is critical to success. Paradoxically, the engagement paradigm requires more involvement from leaders than the current change management paradigm. Leaders play crucial roles throughout the process.

What does shift is the leaders' role. Instead of being responsible for identifying both the problem and the solution, they are now responsible for identifying the issues, purposes, and boundary constraints, and applying the principles of the engagement paradigm to engage others in this dialogue. Throughout the process, leaders concern themselves with the following questions: What needs to change and why? What needs to be different in the organization as a result of our work? What are the boundary conditions? Whose voice needs to be heard? Who else needs to be here? How do we build the necessary connection between people and ideas? How will we create a community of people who are ready and willing to act? How will we embrace democracy throughout the process? The leader's role is not to provide answers to these questions but to ensure that answers are developed.

Leaders are often concerned that if they fully and visibly participate in a change process, employees will not speak out or will blindly accept what the leaders have to say. Similarly, employees are often concerned that if leaders are in the room they will not listen to their concerns. This is exactly the situation that must be corrected. Leaders and employees must learn to work in an atmosphere where there can be a give-and-take of ideas. Employees and leaders need to work together in addressing issues, because each group has information the other does not have. Leaders have a view of what is happening in the outside world and employees have information about what is going on each day within the organization. Both sets of information are necessary to address systemic issues. When leaders follow the principles of the engagement paradigm, they create situations where this kind of information sharing is possible.

Leaders who try to maintain a firewall between the organization and outside stakeholders such as customers, suppliers, and community members typically believe that others will not care the way they do. This fallacy is often given as a reason not to include customers, suppliers, or even people from other parts of the organization in the change process. Accompanying this myth is a fear that if we include outsiders in our change process, we will be airing our dirty laundry in public, thus alienating the very people who are necessary to our success. My experience is just the opposite. Just as including those affected by a change builds ownership and commitment within an organization, it builds ownership and commitment with those outside. As customers and suppliers work with you to build a future, they become invested in your success, becoming true partners in the change process and moving from making demands to offering ideas for mutual gain. It is not uncommon for customers and suppliers to offer ideas about how they could help reduce cost or improve the process as a result of their involvement. At a telephone company my colleagues and I worked with, commercial directory assistance users developed new procedures that benefited both them and the company. In a hospital, doctors, nurses, administrative staff, and insurance companies worked together to improve patient care while reducing unnecessary costs. It is not uncommon for outsiders who have been included in the change process to ask to continue to be part of it because they have become so invested in the outcomes.

The next myth is that productivity will suffer if large numbers of people are involved in the change process. I remember when my colleagues and I first began to talk to leaders about the Conference Model. We would say that we wanted to take hundreds of people off site for two to three days at a time and that we wanted to do this not just once but three or four times! We would look across the table and see people leaning back in their chairs as their eyes rolled. They were calculating the cost of doing this and wondering if it was worth it. What we have seen repeatedly is that productivity does not suffer when more people are involved; in fact, many times it actually improves. We have seen telephone call-handling rates, manufacturing productivity, and customer service levels actually improve during conferences. It turns out that people understand the significance of involving more people in change processes and that those unable to

attend put forth extra effort during these times as a way of supporting those who are attending the conferences.

"The majority cannot be trusted to put the organization's interests
first. Self-interest will take over." The fear accompanying this myth
is that the process will disintegrate. Parts of the organization will try
to improve their departments rather than improving the whole. Similarly, individuals will protect themselves and not make decisions for
the common good. Again, this is contrary to experience. For the most
part, when people understand all the issues and the role they and
their departments play, they are willing to offer ideas and make decisions that benefit the whole. In fact, I have seen people offer up suggestions and ideas that were not in their own self-interest at all
because they were deeply involved in the process and understood the
issues and opportunities. I have even seen people identify their own
jobs as unnecessary! When people are offered the opportunity to be
involved in making difficult decisions rather than having these decisions thrust upon them, the results are often surprising.

The final myth is that it is more cost-effective to put the change
process in the hands of consultants and the best and the brightest
from the organization than to put the change process in the hands
of the many. Certainly, it is costly to widen the circle of involvement,
both financially and emotionally. The whole change process instantly
becomes more visible and the stakes become higher. But what is the
cost of disengagement? What is the cost of brilliant strategies that
never get implemented? What is the cost of change processes that increase cynicism and resistance and provide new material for Dilbert
cartoons? What is the cost of talented people who leave organizations because they believe that their voice does not count? By contrast, throughout this book, you will read stories about organizations
which have made the investment and the benefits they received.

The engagement paradigm is not business as usual. It is not for
the faint of heart and it is not for everyone. Applying the principles
of the engagement paradigm is hard work that requires courage, risk
taking, and perseverance. The reward for these efforts is an organization that is flexible, energetic, innovative, connected, and

responsive enough to meet the demands of a constantly changing business environment.

The Inova Health System Story

Inova Health System is composed of five acute-care hospitals, two long-term care facilities, its region's largest home health service, and behavioral and outpatient services. With fifteen thousand employees and located just eleven miles from Washington, D.C., the Inova System is not immune from the changes affecting health care today, including increasing costs, changes in reimbursement, escalating competition, and the increased need for home and ambulatory care provision. Inova recognized that meeting these challenges required changing the process of patient care delivery. Inova employed a strategy based on the engagement paradigm using both the Future Search Conference and the Conference Model to change its culture, integrate systems, and reduce expenses. In a six-month period, the organization held four conferences six to eight weeks apart. Approximately seven hundred walkthrus were held at all sites around the clock, allowing for thousands of employees (52 percent of the staff) to give their input.

Jolene Tornabeni, executive vice president and chief operating officer, recalls: "I knew there were significant changes that we'd have to go through and I wanted the change driven from the inside out. It was critical for people to be engaged in understanding the need for change, determining what needed to be changed, and designing how it would be changed. I did not want a change strategy that had consultants making recommendations to senior leadership who would then drive the changes down through the system. It is not the way to get ownership and commitment to implementation—it does not work."

Mary Jane Mastorovich, chief nurse executive, recounts the things that kept her up at night during the process: Were the right people in the room? Would people come to the conferences? Would senior leadership support it? Would the system be patient enough to go through the process? Would supporters be able to win over or work with recalcitrant people?

Today patient care redesign is woven into everything that occurs within the Inova System. Multidisciplinary teams called the Collaborative Care Partnership are at its core. Access Management, a centralized, systemwide patient information system, has been developed. Quality Case Management, another new feature, combines the functions of quality, case management, and clinical outcomes into one streamlined service that is linked to the care team. The organization also seeks to promote an internal culture of partnership, accountability, and commitment to learning. Now decision making often happens at the point of service. People in all the individual areas within the organization understand how they contribute to patient care. System integration is happening, and people are sharing and working together across the system. People refer to themselves as Inova employees when previously they referred to themselves by their site's name.

All these changes did not come easily and there is still work to be done. At times, various constituencies in the organization—including doctors, nurses, and middle managers—balked at moving forward. Nevertheless, in the end, sticking with the principles of the engagement paradigm produced a high degree of ownership within the organization. In fact, a doctoral study conducted at the time of the conferences showed that members of the organization had a significantly higher feeling that positive change was going to happen than could be observed in organizations using more traditional methods.

Summary

The engagement paradigm represents a fresh departure from the failing change management paradigm. Shunning mechanistic approaches based solely on techniques that lead to increased cynicism and resistance, the engagement paradigm provides leaders with the four essential principles that lead to an engaged organization: widening the circle of involvement, connecting people to each other, creating communities for action, and embracing democracy. Leaders who adopt these principles find they serve as a polestar as they create the flexible, responsive, innovative organizations necessary in today's world. Adopting the engagement paradigm means leaders must confront five myths that predict loss of control, meddling outsiders, lower productivity, self-interest overwhelming the common good, and excessive cost. Successfully dealing with these myths head-on allows leaders to let go of past practices and fully adopt the engagement paradigm.

PART 2

Producing the Engaged Organization

3

Widening the Circle of Involvement

People and Ideas

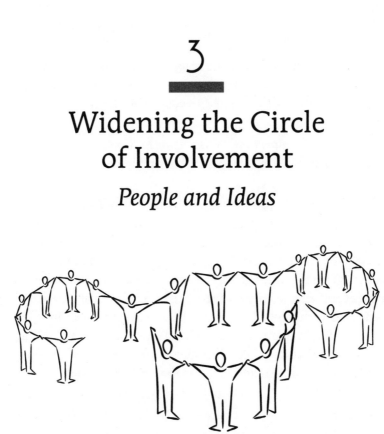

The renowned social scientist Eric Trist said, "Unless we invent ways where paradigm shifts can be experienced by large numbers of people, then change will remain a myth." Marvin Weisbord, who coined the phrase "getting the whole system in the room," further developed this concept. What Weisbord meant was to involve all the various stakeholders of an issue in the deliberations about it. For example, in dealing with complex educational issues, this means including schoolchildren, parents, teachers, and local business and community leaders. In creating organizational futures, this means including employees at all levels, customers, suppliers, and community representatives.

Douglas McGregor supports this point of view in his classic work on *Theory X* and *Theory Y*. McGregor states that the ability to create solutions to organizational issues is widely distributed throughout the organization. It is not the sole province of an elite few, nor is it the province of the best and the brightest, nor does it reside in the hierarchy. Rather, this capacity belongs to the entire organization. Involving the whole system to address systemic issues is at the heart of the engagement paradigm.

In *The Intelligent Advantage: Organizing for Complexity,* Michael D. McMaster provides a final compelling reason for involving more people:

> The personal challenge to those in formal positions of leadership is to see that others have been given an opportunity, a space of possibility—and no more. . . . We become attached to our beliefs that we are leaders because we have titles. . . . These attachments prevent us from showing the way by going first and they support the kind of thinking in which others need to change and we are fine; or these attachments deceive us into believing that we can create all the required change on our own. The worst outcome of this attachment is that we think we are able to know what to change and how to change it without including the rest of the system.

The change management paradigm takes a different approach to the issue of when to involve people in the change process. Initially, the change process is in the hands of the best and the brightest. They develop the plans and strategies and once these plans and strategies are completed, they face the arduous task of creating organizational buy-in. The language they use identifies the problem. *Buy-in* indicates a sales transaction. The sellers create the new initiative and the buyers must be convinced that it is worthy. The engagement paradigm reverses this process by involving large numbers of people in the process from the very beginning. The high level of involvement virtually eliminates the need to sell the product of the change process. Change management produces a few champions, while the engagement paradigm produces hundreds of champions.

I believe that there are three arguments for moving beyond the few to the many when it comes to organizational change. I call these the *ownership/resistance argument,* the *critical-mass argument,* and the *innovation/adaptation/learning argument.* Individually and collectively, these arguments make the case for widening the circle of involvement. Let's delve deeply into these arguments in order to understand them completely.

Increasing Ownership
While Reducing Resistance

Why bother involving more people in the change process? After all, the moment you move beyond yourself and add more people, the whole change process becomes more complicated and less predictable. And as complexity and ambiguity increase, your ability to control the outcome decreases. Who needs the hassle? Isn't it just easier to do it yourself?

It may appear to be easier in the short run to develop change strategies by yourself, but in the long run it is not. Even if you are able to develop a brilliant strategy, you will still have to develop organizational ownership and commitment, and the key to ownership and commitment is to widen the circle of involvement.

When people are excluded from the change process from the very beginning, they rarely exhibit the necessary levels of ownership and commitment to see the change process through to a successful conclusion. Even when the committees of the parallel organization (operating under the change management paradigm) seek input from the organization members through interviews and other data-gathering mechanisms, this process rarely produces the level of ownership necessary for success. The level of ownership that is created when people are asked for input pales in comparison to the level of ownership achieved when people are involved in creating and developing the change strategy.

The reverse side of ownership is resistance. Not only do those who are excluded from the change process not own it in the same way as those who develop it, they are often actively resistant. In their classic 1948 article, "Overcoming Resistance to Change," Coch and French describe the impact of involving people in changes that affect them. Coch and French conducted experiments on the effect of involving employees in changing work procedures in a manufacturing organization. They found that by including employees in the change process from the very beginning, they were able to reduce resistance to the new work procedures. High-involvement groups, in which employees were involved from the beginning, not only outperformed the no-participation groups, they also experienced increased productivity while the no-participation group's productivity dropped and grievances and quits increased. Today these results seem intuitively obvious, yet we often ignore the lessons learned from this landmark study. Exclusion produces resistance. Inclusion produces ownership.

In a situation quite similar to the one that Detroit Edison faced, a manufacturing organization had been working for over three years to redesign its workforce with little to show for the effort. The union-management steering committee was engaged, but few other employees were involved. Recognizing that market factors could put the company out of business if they did not make the needed changes quickly, its leaders decided to engage the organization in creating a new organizational design. They used the Conference Model process to engage the whole organization through a series of three 3-day conferences (250 people per conference), and then conducted walkthrus for those unable to attend. Using conferences and walkthrus, everyone had input into the new organization as it was being created. In a few short months, they had moved from apathy to interest and from a few supporters to a critical mass of people who cared about the outcomes. Coincidentally, as this process unfolded, productivity began to increase and employees began to set new production records even before they implemented any of the improvements they identified during the conference process.

Creating a Critical Mass of People

The second argument for widening the circle of involvement is the effect of creating a critical mass for change. In sociological terms, *critical mass* is defined as that group of people necessary for an idea to be adopted by the whole population. For example, for smoking or

HOW TO INCREASE OWNERSHIP WHILE REDUCING RESISTANCE

Involve the many in the change process from the very beginning. Do not assume that because someone is a representative for a particular point of view, organizational role, or unit that others who are not part of the discussion will feel that they are represented or will support the outcomes. Provide opportunities for direct involvement through orientations, town-hall meetings, walkthrus, feedback sessions, intranets, and large group conferences.

Make sure that leaders at all levels of the organization are included in the process from the very beginning. Engagement is not just for lower-level employees; it is for everyone. Many change processes bypass leaders in their zeal to involve lower-level employees—thus creating unnecessary resistance. Leaders are like everyone else; when they are not included, their resistance increases. Employees usually trust the most the information they get from their immediate supervisor about what is going on in the organization. When leaders at all levels are involved in the process from the very beginning, they are more likely to support the process. When they are not, they often respond to questions about what is happening by saying something like, "Beats me, no one ever tells me what's happening."

Remember that open resistance is natural, and it serves a very useful role in the change process. As resistance is voiced, issues and concerns surface. When these issues and concerns are taken into account, outcomes improve. The key to reducing resistance is putting yourself in other people's shoes and seeing the world through their eyes. When this happens a new level of understanding occurs. The person who is seen as resisting becomes a person with real concerns and issues. Often, this level of understanding produces new options. Even when new solutions do not become available, the feeling of being understood by others increases a person's willingness to give a new idea a chance.

driving after consuming alcohol to become unfashionable, a critical mass of the population has to denounce these practices. This critical mass then influences the rest of the population.

Critical mass is sometimes said to range between 10 percent and 30 percent of a population, but I believe that successful organizational change requires a critical mass of at least 20 percent to 40 percent of all employees. When you look at top-down strategies and the current change management paradigm, it is readily apparent that they fail to involve enough people to produce a critical mass for change, thus dooming the change process from the very beginning. Even considering the many people that the change management paradigm enrolls after key decisions and strategies are developed, this paradigm does not produce a critical mass of people with sufficient ownership of the issues to care about the outcomes.

You can describe the membership of an organization about to embark on a change process as a bell-shaped curve. On one tail of the curve are those people who will readily adopt the change because they are predisposed to accept new directions. On the other tail are those who are predisposed to reject the change, even if it benefits them. In the middle are the undecideds. They can move toward either tail of the curve. Developing a critical mass means creating a group of people who will influence the middle of the curve. You can't do this by selecting ahead of time who these people will be, but you can create inclusive processes for the whole organization and let the critical mass emerge.

Increasing Innovation, Adaptation, and Learning

The third and most compelling argument for widening the circle of involvement comes from the study of complex adaptive systems. For those of you who may have felt that the ownership/resistance argument and the critical-mass argument were too people-oriented, this argument provides scientific evidence for involving more people in the change process.

HOW TO CREATE
A CRITICAL MASS OF PEOPLE

Creating a critical mass is about moving from the few to the many. Here are some questions and guidelines that will help you create a critical mass of people.

Ask yourself the following questions: Who else needs to be here? Whose voice needs to heard?

When thinking about who to involve, use the following criteria:

• Information: Ask people to participate if they have information that will be needed to create effective solutions. For example, include those who have specific knowledge about the new information system that is going to be introduced.

• Impact: Choose people who will be directly or indirectly affected by the changes that are being considered. For example, in a school system, include students in the process; in a business, include employees from the various units and functions where the change will be implemented.

• Authority: Choose people who have the authority to implement potential changes. For example, include the leader or leaders who must ultimately approve the changes being recommended.

• Responsibility: Invite those who have responsibility for the outcomes to participate in the change process. For example, include the supervisors and middle managers who will have operational responsibility for the proposed changes.

• Opposition: Invite those likely to be opposed to the new course of action. For example, include those whose jobs might be eliminated by the proposed changes.

Recently a whole new school of scientific thought called *complex adaptive systems* has been developed at the Santa Fe Institute. Located in Santa Fe, New Mexico, the institute is composed of a group of scientists, economists, computer geniuses, and Nobel laureates. Their approach is based on studying what appear on the surface to be a set of unrelated sciences, including condensed-matter physics, evolutionary biology, computer science, political science, economics, sociology, psychology, and history. Part of their work involves using these diverse fields to try to understand what happens in systems where there are many different actions being carried out by many different people in a constantly changing environment. Their work involves going beyond simple cause-and-effect analysis of presumably static environments to developing frameworks for understanding systems where there are many different actors, with varying strategies, in increasingly turbulent environments.

What does the work of the Santa Fe Institute have to do with organizations? It was not so long ago that organizational theorists believed that environments in which organizations found themselves were uniform and unchanging. They also believed organizational change was based on simple cause and effect: if you purchase more efficient equipment, productivity will increase. Leaders in today's world know these assumptions no longer hold. Organizations find themselves in increasingly complex markets and political environments. And anyone who has ever tried to improve productivity by purchasing more efficient equipment knows that reaching the expected productivity gains requires far more than simply unpacking and starting the equipment.

Moreover, organizations today have to be able to deal with multiple change initiatives simultaneously. It is not uncommon for an organization to be introducing new information systems, reengineering various processes, and attempting to transform itself from a hierarchical silo-based organization to a cooperative team-based organization all at the same time.

When applied to organizational settings, the study of complex adaptive systems provides leaders with an alternative framework that is nonlinear and addresses the complexity of their world. It is particularly relevant here because these concepts help us to understand how widening the circle of involvement affects innovation, adaptation and learning.

In *Harnessing Complexity,* Robert Axelrod—noted political scientist, game theoretician, and creator of the tit-for-tat theory (and my cousin; it isn't often that an author gets to cite a member of his own family)—and co-author Michael Cohen define complex adaptive systems as follows:

> When a system contains agents [in the organizational context, people] or populations [groups of people] that seek to adapt, we use the term Complex Adaptive System. If agents change strategies as a result of the actions of other agents, the system becomes much more complex, and prediction becomes more difficult. In a Complex Adaptive System, everyone's strategies influence the context in which everyone else is acting. . . . A system is complex when there are strong interactions among its elements, so that current events heavily influence the probabilities of many kinds of later events.

Given this definition, organizations are most certainly complex adaptive systems. But what does the study of such systems offer to organizations and leaders? I believe that it offers new insights into the world in which organizations now find themselves. The old belief that organizations were linear, cause-and-effect-driven systems living in static environments is outdated. Monetary crises halfway around the globe can cause shock waves in businesses across the United States. The product life cycle in the computer industry is measured in months instead of years, as organizations deal with constantly changing technology and fickle consumers. The entire health care delivery system is in a constant state of flux as physicians, hospitals, and insurers struggle to deal with a world of mindboggling technological advances, changing patient expectations, and escalating costs. Organizations are constantly seeking ways to adapt in order to survive in an increasingly turbulent environment. Axelrod and Cohen provide a framework for working with these issues. They state that you harness complexity when you stop asking the typical cause-and-effect questions and begin asking a new set of questions: What agents and strategies are involved? and What interventions might create new combinations or destroy old ones?

These and other concepts of complex adaptive systems help explain how widening the circle of involvement increases innovation, adaptation, learning, as well as how it enlarges conceptual space. They also help illuminate the reasons why silo organizations and current change strategies combine to prevent these benefits from occurring.

Innovation

Most people have a picture of innovation that shows the scientist who, working alone in the laboratory, makes a breakthrough discovery. On the face of it, this would argue that involving more people does not produce innovation, it works against it. However, this is not the case. Innovation occurs through exposure to new and different ideas, ways of thinking, and ways of doing things. Working with people who are similar to yourself only reinforces your current ways of thinking. Moreover, it turns out that even the most dedicated scientist was not alone after all. He or she probably had thousands of conversations and shared experiments with others before coming up with the breakthrough concept.

Complex adaptive systems look at innovation from the perspective of variety. Axelrod and Cohen state that unless variety is introduced into a system, innovation and adaptation are unlikely. Variety is introduced into a system by providing opportunities for people with varying points of view and strategies for dealing with issues to meet and interact with one another. It is through these encounters that new ways of doing things are invented and eventually adopted by the system. Without this type of interaction—which can only come from widening the circle of involvement—innovation is not possible.

McMaster suggests that involving more people supports innovation because it increases everyone's concept of what is possible. "A particular individual's view of what's possible may be larger than that of some community of which he or she is not a part. However, if that individual is part of the community, the community view of what is possible will include theirs and will always be larger than the individual view. If dialogue occurs, the community will expand and be larger than the sum of the individual views."

Everyone's concept of what is possible increases when people at all levels of the organization and important outside stakeholders such as customers, suppliers, and community officials are included. Discussing issues with those who are part of the same system but who have different perspectives sows the seeds of innovation. It is readily apparent that when change emanates from a single source, as with a top-down management style, or from like-minded people such as groups of senior executives, these strategies will lack the variety necessary for innovative thought.

My colleagues and I make extensive use of these concepts to increase innovation when we conduct large group sessions. Here are two short examples, one from our workshop called Essential Skills of Engaging and Convening and the second from our Design Conference (a large group session for redesigning organizations).

At the five-day Essential Skills for Engaging and Convening workshop, teams from organizations come together with the goal of developing a strategy for engaging their organization in change. These teams come with real projects. Their goal is twofold: to learn the principles of engaging and convening and to leave the workshop with a strategy for their particular change process. Variety is introduced into the system in two powerful ways. First, the workshop is conducted by three different consulting firms, The Axelrod Group, Vista Consulting, and 5 Oceans Consulting. Because these firms have different approaches to the engagement paradigm, the design of the workshop reflects the different orientations and is far more innovative than the predecessor to this workshop, which was developed by my firm alone. Second, participants meet in three different modalities: mixed groups containing members from the various teams in attendance, their own organizational teams, and as a total community. Typically, mixed groups work on activities that deepen the learning, the departmental teams apply the learning to their projects, and the total community explores the growth and development of the group as a whole.

Another unique feature is the use of a planning committee. At the end of each day, the workshop leaders and a small group of participants, usually one or two members from each team, meet to review the day's events and the workshop's objectives. During this pulse-taking session, we ask the fundamental questions: What is working? What is not working? What do we have to do differently to meet our goals? The group reviews the agenda for the next day and makes necessary adjustments. The next day, the planning committee reports its data to the total community and shares the changes that were developed. Each night a different group of people meets and goes through the same process.

In our Design Conference, we use variety in the following manner: First, the group in attendance represents a wide circle of involvement. Second, during the course of the session, participants meet in three different mixed groups: one group includes representatives of the various constituencies present, another includes only members of a specific department, and the third is large group sessions. Additionally, these large group sessions also use a version of the previously described planning-committee process.

The Design Conference (typically three days) starts out by giving participants in mixed groups the task of designing an organization based on a single criterion, which is different for each group. Then new mixed groups are formed and they analyze the previously developed designs in terms of their positive, negative, and interesting aspects. This data is shared with the larger group to make the results of analyses available to everyone. Then participants join a new mixed group to create a new design that uses the best of all the ideas developed and that meets all the criteria for the new organization. Again these design proposals are analyzed and the results are shared with the total community. Groups adjust their designs and the designs are again shared with the total community. Then the total community goes through a multi-voting process to determine the final design. To ensure that good ideas are not lost, a Treasure Hunt process is introduced: having chosen a final design, participants are asked to identify features from the designs that were not chosen that they want to see included in the final design.

Notice what is going on in these two examples. Variety is introduced into the system in a number of ways:

■ Workshop leaders who come from different orientations produce innovation in the workshop design.
■ The pulse-taking of the planning committee provides the information necessary to make adjustments.
■ Planning committees made up of both workshop leaders and participants continue the process of introducing variety into the workshop design.
■ Rotating the membership of the planning committee throughout the workshop ensures that it does not become stagnant.
■ The review sessions that start each day, in which the planning committee shares how it used the pulse data to make changes in the agenda, continues the information loop and produces trust.
■ The extensive use of mixed groups and rotating memberships in the Design Conference introduce variety into the system.
■ The Treasure Hunt process makes sure that good ideas are not lost.

The variety these processes introduce into the system increases the probability that innovation and creativity will occur. By contrast, the current change management paradigm does not connect enough people throughout the system to spark innovation. In fact, one of the core problems with this structure is its failure to create communication links between the various committees so that information can be shared and so that innovations promote the common good. What we often see in these instances are innovations that make a particular unit or department better while at the same time causing trouble for other units or departments—suboptimizing the whole.

Adaptation

Adaptation refers to the ability of the organization to respond to rapidly changing conditions in its environment. Adaptation occurs when the various parts of the system are able to encounter each other and either copy successful strategies or develop new strategies because of their interaction. Today's structured hierarchical organizations work against adaptation because communication and coordination is made difficult by organizational boundaries, overly rigid chains of command, strict job descriptions, and communication protocols, all of which reduce the system's ability to react to rapidly changing conditions. When we widen the circle of involvement, we create connections between people and ideas. Thus it becomes possible for people who are facing the same issues but are working in different departments to come together and develop systemic solutions. When interaction and communication is regimented through silo command-and-control structures, adaptive processes die.

A common experience for many people in organizations is to come together at a retreat or workshop where the traditional blocks to organizational communication are removed. Informality is the name of the game. Titles do not matter, everyone is on a first name basis, people interact across levels and functions, and everyone is excited about what they are talking about and the ease at which things can be accomplished. Then it's time to go back to work. Participants leave full of enthusiasm only to return to their organizational silos, cubicles, and offices—where the energy from the off-site meeting quickly dissipates. They have moved back into the old organizational structure where communication across levels and functions is difficult. For a while they try to overcome these barriers, but soon it becomes too difficult to surmount the impediments to working across functions and levels, and the organization settles back into its old patterns. The off-site meeting becomes a distant memory and the seeds of disillusionment begin to grow.

When parts of the organization attempt to resolve systemic issues from their own myopic perspective, they inevitably fail because they lack the perspective of the other components of the system. When leaders meet with leaders, they develop solutions that make sense from the leaders' point of view. When lower-level employees meet with other lower-level employees, they develop solutions that support their point of view. In addition, when customers meet only with other customers, they develop customer-oriented solutions. When we widen the circle of involvement to include all of the system's many viewpoints, we create the possibility for systemic solutions, solutions that benefit the whole instead of the parts. This is not possible when top-down strategies are employed. While the change management paradigm moves in the right direction, it fails to take on a systemic perspective.

Again, McMaster provides some guidance: "Innovation and creativity occur where information from the chaotic 'external world' meets the structured information of the internal world. Creativity is the process of making new meanings in the combining of these two domains." Innovation cannot occur when we separate organizational members from customers and each other. A chemical products company recognized this fact when it involved customers and employees from all the various components of the organization in developing a new product-development process. Because of their successful interactions in developing the new process, scientists from the lab, production people, and sales people now routinely meet with customers to understand their needs and create new products. The organization is now able to adapt rapidly to shifts in customer requirements because both the scientists in the lab and the manufacturing people are fully engaged in product development. The previously held belief was that the only people who had enough social skills to meet with customers were the sales force!

Learning

Since Peter Senge's book *The Fifth Discipline* came out, much has been made of "the learning organization." Unfortunately, many organizations have jumped on the learning-organization bandwagon and trivialized this important concept by equating learning with training.

And in doing so, they equate creating a learning organization with creating a corporate university—a larger, more sophisticated training organization. But training is not learning. Training is about facts, figures, and processes. Learning is the process of continually identifying what is working and what is not working and making the necessary corrections. From the perspective of complex adaptive systems, learning is the way in which the results of this constant inquiry about what is working and not working become internalized in the system so that the system can adapt to a constantly changing environment.

The other day I had a conversation with my son, David—a professional ski instructor—about how people learn to ski. As the conversation developed, we posed the following situation: What if the way you taught people to ski was to sit them in a classroom and have them study all the principles and mechanics of skiing, and then put them out on the slopes and say, "Ski!" The results in terms of traumatized psyches and broken body parts are predictable. The process of learning to ski is one of constantly identifying what is working and not working and making adjustments to deal with constantly changing conditions. A beginning skier experiences skiing as both awkward and frightening. However, if the skier keeps asking these questions and has the support of a good coach (remember how Hewlett-Packard used coaches to support leadership changes?), they will eventually reach the point at which skiing becomes internalized. David puts it this way: "Skiing for me is no different from walking. I don't even have to think about it." At this point a skier has embodied the lessons of skiing and has really learned to ski. However, this all hinges on asking the fundamental questions of what is working, what is not working, and what has to be done differently.

Learning is crucial to the survival of an organization. What I mean by learning is not individual learning but the ability of the whole system to learn from its experiences and then use that learning to adapt to its environment. Art Kleiner has developed a whole process called "learning histories" that engages the organization in the exploration of current and past experiences with change so that the total system can learn. For systemic learning to occur, widening the circle of involvement is essential for two reasons. First, involving more people increases the opportunities to learn from others' experiences. Second, involving more people enhances the probability that learning will occur throughout the system.

The Mercy Story

At Mercy Healthcare in Sacramento, California, my colleagues and I used the following approach to support learning as we implemented a new organizational design that was developed using the Conference Model. The problem facing us was that we had five hospitals that were part of the redesign process. The new design called for both systemic and local changes. Some changes affected the whole organization and required concurrent implementation across the system, and other changes applied only to a specific hospital.

To facilitate learning, we created an implementation planning group. This group was composed of key people from all the systems and hospitals involved. We had a rotating membership so that the units or systems that were undergoing the implementation process had the most members and those who had either already implemented the changes or were about to implement the changes had fewer members. This process allowed learning to flow from those who went before to those who were next. Large group processes were used extensively during the implementation process to adapt the redesign template to local conditions and to share experiences. The rotating membership of the planning group and the extensive use of large group conferences provided a mechanism for sharing learning as the implementation process proceeded. This in turn allowed the organization to adjust the implementation process to conditions that could not have been foreseen when the implementation process began. Instead of sticking to a rigid plan, the organization adapted its plan as learning was occurring during implementation. This could not have occurred without widening the circle of involvement.

Change processes that lay out a clear path are seductive in that they promise a step-by-step approach with clear outcomes and results. They appeal to the common human need for predictability, order, and structure. However, when change processes do not build in mechanisms to self-correct and learn, they are doomed to failure, because they do not provide for adaptation and learning as the process unfolds. It is impossible for organizational change to occur without ever deviating from the original plan. Eisenhower said it best when he described the planning process necessary for a military campaign. He said you must develop detailed plans for conducting the campaign and then be prepared to abandon them at a moment's notice.

For learning of this nature to occur, it is crucial to widen the circle of involvement. When organizational levels or departments conduct discussions among themselves about what is working or not working, they often degenerate into blaming the groups that are not present. *If only the other group would get their act together. If only they were as smart as we are. If only they would do what we want them to do.* This kind of thinking does not produce learning that leads to innovation and an ability to adapt to ever-changing conditions; rather, it closes the borders to broader communication and interaction.

Enlarging Conceptual Space

Bringing more people into the conversation is essential, but equally important is increasing the depth of the conversation. When you widen the circle of involvement, you also widen the conversation by enlarging the conceptual space. You enlarge the discussion when there are opportunities for sharing information, discussing the issues, implementing predetermined plans, and co-creating initiatives. Conceptual space is increased as you move from discussions about your particular job to discussions about your work group, your organization, and finally the system itself.

Conceptual space is at its widest point when people are involved in the process from the very beginning. They are then able to understand the issues, develop initiatives, and implement them. In these types

HOW TO INCREASE INNOVATION, ADAPTATION, AND LEARNING

When variety is introduced into a system, the probability that innovation, adaptation, and learning will occur increases. Here are some ways to increase variety in a system.

Include people from outside the formal system. This means including customers, suppliers, citizens, patients in hospital settings, and students in educational settings. Here I advocate going beyond just interviewing them or inviting them to be part of a panel discussion and then leave. Rather, I urge you to invite them to be full partners with you as you discuss the issues and identify new courses of action.

Include those who may think differently from the way you do. For example, you could include musicians, artists, and educators to discuss technical issues. Because their professional training is different from yours, they will bring a different discipline and thought process to the situation.

Do not handpick all the participants. The first choice of many leaders, handpicking all the participants reduces variety. It's much more effective to use a selection process that gives equal opportunity for everyone to participate while holding to a minimum the number of people who are specifically asked to participate either because of the position they hold or the knowledge they possess. I will say more about this in Chapter Six. For now, it is enough to remember that processes that end up populated with the same cast of characters, those who are always asked to contribute, do not increase innovation, adaptation, and learning—new thinking is not being introduced into the system.

Adding new people to existing groups or rotating membership in existing groups is another way of introducing variety.

People with new and different ways of looking at things provide fresh insights and ideas, causing group members to take into account differing points of view.

When conducting larger group sessions or meetings that require more than a few people, create discussion groups that represent the maximum mix of people present to ensure variety. On the other hand, you can use homogenous groups—people from the same level, department, point of view—when you want to understand a subject from a particular perspective or when you want to get to a level of detail that requires specific knowledge and expertise.

of discussions, the glass is not only full but overflowing. Ownership and commitment are the highest and the benefits of the engagement paradigm come to fruition.

Here is an example of what happens when conceptual space is enlarged. An Air Force base was in the midst of a major reengineering process. In spite of the fact that a consulting firm had sought the input of many people in the organization through committees and focus groups, there were still deep pockets of resistance. Something more was required to ensure the success of the project. And so organization leaders used the four principles of the engagement paradigm to engage the organization in the implementation of the new processes and procedures. The project was to be released in stages, and for the major releases of the project they held large group sessions in which people could come together to understand what was going to happen, identify potential pitfalls, and identify solutions. Attending these sessions were government contractors, air force and navy personnel, and union officials, as well as the consultants who were working on the project. The results were astounding. In the words of the lead consultant, "During our large group session we identified and developed solutions for all the issues where I thought the project was vulnerable. I wish we had had this kind of involvement from the very beginning. The whole process would have been a whole lot easier."

HOW TO ENLARGE CONCEPTUAL SPACE

Information sharing is probably the most popular form of increasing conceptual space. In many organizations, this is done through media and employee meetings. A typical employee meeting consists of a leader speaking for 90 percent of the allotted time and answering questions 10 percent of the time. The interaction, if there is any, is between the leader and the audience. In most cases, there are few questions. The design of the meeting (which one organization I worked with describes as "sit and get") prevents interaction among those assembled, which in turn limits the chance that anything will occur as a result of the meeting.

One step up from information-sharing meetings is actual discussion about the issues. Instead of people just passively receiving information, participants are engaged in discussing the issues and their meaning.

The next step is discussions in which people are asked to implement a predetermined strategy or plan. This provides employees with a classic opportunity to see the glass half empty or half full. Even though people may not have contributed to the initial planning of the changes, they may be able to develop ownership and commitment by figuring out how to make the strategy work in their part of the organization. On the other hand, they may resent the changes developed by others and actively resist implementing them.

Conceptual space is at its widest when people are able to both identify the issues and develop courses of action. Obviously, there are always constraints regarding resources, time, and money and these boundaries need to be identified ahead of time. Limiting boundaries to the few that really matter allows individuals, groups, and organizations to enlarge conceptual space so that they understand all the dangers and opportunities and consequently develop creative, innovative responses.

A question that always comes up with this type of meeting is who should attend. Should you hold meetings for specific organizational units, or should the meeting be populated with people within various parts of the organization? The answer is that if you want to create a situation in which a wide variety of viewpoints are present, then the mixed department meeting is the best. However, if you want to delve deeply into a departmental issue, then the departmental strategy is the best.

The Southern Cross University Story

Two Senior Lecturers step on stage. One is juggling a tray piled with cups like a house of cards and the other is wearing six hats. "Why are you wearing all those hats?" says the first to the second. "Well," he says, beginning to remove the hats one by one, "this comfy one's my research hat, this very large one's my teaching hat, this scruffy one's my community-service hat, this boring one's my academic-governance hat, this spotty one's my course-development hat, this very long one is my student-support hat, and . . . [at this point all the hats tumble to the floor] this last, tiny hat is my home life." Ruefully he concludes, "I guess I'm trying to wear just too many hats! But, hey, why are you juggling that tray of cups?" [at which point they suddenly sway out of control and start to crash to the floor]. "Aargh, I've just got too much on my plate!"

The audience of more than a hundred fellow academics, senior administrators, students, and external stakeholders from Southern Cross University roars with laughter. They are appreciating the clever way their colleagues have captured one of the main themes to have emerged for debate—the diverse, often unreasonable, set of expectations academics place on themselves or find that others have placed on them in this fiercely competitive, post-Dawkins world in higher education. But all of them have had their own turn on stage presenting their dramatized versions of problems they feel need to be solved or norms they want challenged. This is just one activity in a series of conferences in the engagement paradigm, which they are using to design a new university.

Established in 1993, Southern Cross is Australia's second smallest and youngest university. Based in Lismore on the north coast of New South Wales, it has a smaller campus in Coffs Harbour and centers in several other towns in the region. In early 1996, it had about 500 staff and 5,500 students. It brings nearly $160 million into the local region every year. Its survival and success is obviously of vital importance to all its stakeholders.

And yet its survival is by no means assured. Economic and industrial deregulation, cyberspace availability of education from just about anywhere in the world via the Internet, the decline in student demand for places and the recent rise of demanding consumerism in all fields, together with its rural location, mean that SCU's future is certainly not secure.

During the long and frustrating enterprise-wide bargaining process in 1994 and 1995, the future facing the university was often addressed, but almost always in such a way that it left the parties further divided. The bargaining logjam was broken when the university sent three union and three management members of the bargaining group to the Workplace Australia Conference on workplace reform held in Melbourne in May, 1995. Here they gained fresh insight into what workplace reform could be, they learned how best-practice unionism and management looked, *and* they met me and my wife. From us, the SCU team learned of the process we had developed to aid organizational renewal.

Three weeks later, a bargaining agreement was completed—an apparent miracle given the preceding months of fruitless negotiation. Included was a clause outlining the parties' commitment to jointly managing organizational reform processes so that there would be "collegiate involvement of the persons who will be affected by change in its planning and implementation." To make this happen, a committee with three management and three union representatives was established called the Collegiate Organizational Reform Committee (CORC).

From the first planning meeting of the CORC in late November to the final approval, this highly participative analysis and redesign process took four months. Over 40 percent of the staff was directly involved, together with a significant number of students and other clients of the university. One of the spin-off benefits was the opportunity for enhanced relationships to be created between people from different parts and levels of the university. Staff-student relations particularly benefited.

There is no doubt that the major benefit is the speed with which the university went from the vice-chancellor's recognition of the need for restructuring to a quite different structural arrangement that had broad institutional support. As implementation now proceeds (more slowly to take account of the need to keep the business of the university going), those directly affected in each area are fine-tuning how the overall direction will be put into practice.

Several stakeholder groups that are usually excluded from these kinds of change were especially delighted with the process. These included students and indigenous people, many of whom reported that they felt listened to and empowered in ways they had never before experienced. This feeling was shared by the relatively junior administrative staff. They reported their satisfaction at being able to sit down together and share their hopes, concerns, and ideas for the future of their workplace.

As well as the boost to morale engendered by this sense of inclusiveness, the fifty-four hours of conferences generated literally hundreds of ideas for improvement. These have been clustered and plans have been made to follow up on them. These plans have been published, enabling everyone to keep track of progress on their specific issues. The ideas range from the requirements for a new management information system to ways of maintaining the enhanced cross-boundary relationships between different levels and groupings.

Finally, the active involvement of some participants who represent the university's customers—enterprises that have purchased services— has undoubtedly enhanced its reputation for care and customer focus within its marketplace. Within the new structural arrangements, these customers and students will now be able to contribute their views on the quality of existing courses and their delivery as well as on the nature of any proposed new courses. In the extremely competitive field of higher education, this last benefit may turn out to be the most important of all.

Summary

The first principle foundational to the engagement paradigm is widening the circle of involvement. Three arguments for widening the circle of involvement include increasing ownership and reducing resistance—the more people are involved in the design of the changes, the more they own the outcomes, creating a critical mass for change. Significant change requires more than just a few people who care about the outcomes, it requires a critical mass increasing innovation, adaptation, and learning. And introducing variety into a system increases the probability that these key benefits will occur.

Widening the circle of involvement also enlarges an organization's conceptual space, allowing more and better ideas to arise. These arguments cannot be answered by the current change management paradigm. In the next chapter, I will move beyond widening the circle of involvement to creating communities that care about the outcomes and are ready and willing to act.

4

Connecting People
to Each Other

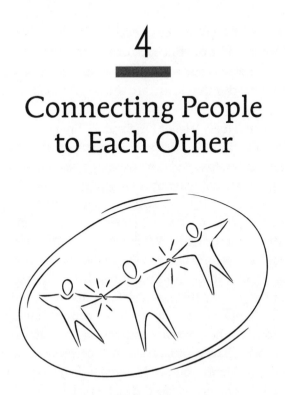

Widening the circle of involvement as described in Chapter Three
brings more people into the conversation, but unless they are
able to connect to the purpose and with each other, they will
be unable to act. In this chapter, I will take up the issue of connecting
people to each other and discuss ways to create both connections between people and a compelling purpose.

The Importance of Connection

Connection is part of the human condition. Whenever we find ourselves in a new situation, we seek to connect with others. We instantly
try to find something in common with the other person, be it a

common interest, an acquaintance, or a geographical location. Finding connections helps us to feel safe in new situations. We connect through our heads (logic), our hearts (emotions), and our hands (experience). Not everyone connects in the same way: some of us connect through ideas or concepts, others through common beliefs and values, still others through an experience of working together. Here are three stories that illustrate the importance of connection:

"Hi! My name is Joe." "Hello! I'm Sarah." "I'm Robert." As the introductions continue, you desperately try to associate names with faces. Panic sets in. *How will I ever remember who is who?* Thirty seconds later, you cannot remember anyone's name.

There you are, coffee in hand, appearing serene while you frantically search for connection. Then you formulate your strategy. The questions come rapidly. Where did you go to school? Where have you worked before? Oh, you live in Colorado. Are you a skier? With each question you hope to hit pay dirt, to break the chasm that separates you and the nameless faces that stand opposite you. And then it happens. You find the connection. Someone in the group is from your hometown, another works in a similar field, and you and another have mutual friends. The iceberg of isolation begins to melt. Suddenly, you can remember their names. They have gone from being nameless faces to being real people. The tenuous first links of connection are forged.

The fury of the hurricane hits. No electricity, no water, and sand and seaweed are strewn over what was once the living room of your oceanfront property. Your car is found two miles away, turned on its side by the intensity of the storm. Trees sever rooftops, leaving cutaway houses. Your family album floats away and joins your neighbors' artifacts in a debris-laden stream that carries them down to the ocean. Yet out of this disaster, connection is born. Your neighbors check in to see if you are all right. They bring food and water, readily sharing their meager resources. You see a tree down and along with others, lift it from the house where it rests. Another neighbor with a boat takes an elderly man to the hospital over the washed-out roads. People who the day before barely gave each other the time of day are now sharing food, clothing, and shelter.

You look around the room and see a group of people in whom your trust runs deep. No matter what happens next, you know that the heartfelt connection you have with these people will never be broken. No matter where you are, a call from one of them will cause you to stop whatever you are doing and respond immediately. The last six months have been pure hell. But the long hours, impossible deadlines, demanding leaders, and shifting customer requirements have built a level of connection between you that can never be destroyed. There were knock-down-drag-out fights, times you thought the group would split apart at the seams, yet you did more than survive, you succeeded beyond everyone's wildest dreams. And in the process, you became friends.

As human beings we know that connection makes a difference. When we connect, we build trust, and when we build trust, we are able to create synergy. Whether learning more about another person or coming together to respond to a natural disaster or working together to achieve an organizational goal, connection makes it possible. When we join with other people, we not only feel more human, we are able to do greater things than we could have done alone. We move beyond the isolation of our locked doors, gated communities, office cubicles, and organizational silos to unite with others.

The theme song from the TV sitcom *Cheers* suggests that we all want to be in a place where everybody knows our name. Even more, we want to be with people who care about us. The bar Cheers was a safe haven in a cold and isolated world. But in today's organizations, people work together for years without ever even meeting. Their communications consist of voice mail, fax, and e-mail. Their isolation is reinforced by walls, cubicles, and organizational silos. When they need to get something done, they do not know where to go or whom to ask. This lack of connection reinforces the silo mentality and the negative stereotypes about that "other" department, the one that can never get its act together.

Even proponents of electronic forms of connection such as e-mail and Web-based conferencing state that these processes work better when the participants have established a relationship prior to using high-tech communications. Our ability to work successfully in a high-tech environment is enhanced by high touch. Connection, establishing a bond with another human being, promotes collaboration.

Sometimes it is the cause that connects us, such as Mothers Against Drunk Driving. We come together because we know that what we are doing will make a difference (such as saving teenage lives) that is larger than ourselves. In working toward this higher purpose, we get to know people. We see them in action. We hear them speak out. We learn their strengths and weaknesses. It is through this process of working together toward a higher purpose that bonds of connection are forged.

In other instances connection precedes purpose. We meet people professionally or socially and find common interests. We think to ourselves, someday I would like to work with that person. And then suddenly we find ourselves in a new job, or charged with a new responsibility, and there we are sitting in a room with new associates who nevertheless have familiar faces. Because of our previous connections, we feel safe and secure. We like these people, trust them, and feel we can make it happen.

Connection is the oil that lubricates the squeaky wheels of organizational life. Everyone knows that when you are working with someone with whom you feel a connection, the work is not only easier but better. And so it is curious that spending time developing connections is seen as superfluous, a necessary evil rather than an essential component of change.

Nearly every model of group development and formation has connection as its first stage. Whether the stages are forming, norming, and storming, or inclusion, control, and openness, connection is the foundational step. Yet this is the stage that we often rush, ignore, or eliminate altogether.

Harrison Owen, the creator of Open Space Technology, recognized the importance of connection and it became the cornerstone of his process for engaging an organization in change. Owen noticed that whenever he went to meetings people reported that the most valuable parts of the sessions occurred during the coffee breaks, lunches, and other unscheduled activities. During these informal times, people connected with each other, got to know each other as people, and discussed issues of mutual interest. Noticing this, Owen created a change process whose very foundation is people connecting and working with each other on issues of mutual interest and concern.

The other day the president of a union local said: "What surprised me the most is that, when you get right down to it, we all want the same thing." He had just completed a joint union-management workshop to plan how to engage the organization in a major change process. During the workshop, members of each group began to connect, moving beyond stereotypes to understand each other as people. As the parties discussed their interests in the future of the organization, they were genuinely surprised by how many interests they had in common. It was in everyone's interest that the organization grow and prosper, that the organization produce a quality product, that employees be properly trained and have a safe environment to work in, and that the organization meet customer requirements. These discoveries would not have been possible if the parties had not increased their connections with each other. When connection increases, trust increases. Connecting people to each other is the foundation for building communities for action. Without connection, communities do not exist.

An organization wanted to use a high-involvement process to support the implementation of a new information system. It widened the circle of involvement by including people from all departments and functions, as well as customers, suppliers, and union officials. However, when it came time to schedule sessions for creating connection in the group, the managers balked. They saw themselves holding a pep rally rather than connecting people to each other and to the purpose. There is a fundamental difference between holding a pep rally and building connections. The goal of a pep rally is to build energy and excitement among those who show up so that they will cheer and support the cause the following day. They are not expected to work together, to make changes, or produce anything new. Their role is one of support. When you build connections between people, you are laying the foundation for engaging people in a change process that will require them to create a future and take coordinated actions to make that future a reality. In order to engage people in making the new information system work, this organization had to move beyond holding pep rallies to engaging people in the processes of making the new system work.

Announcing a new direction does not make it so, nor does it connect people to that direction. For people to connect to a new direction, they need time to chew on it, digest it, and make it their own. This does not occur in one-way conversations. Recently I observed a leader speak to her organization about her vision for the future. People were seated auditorium-style to receive the word. She spoke for over half an hour. At the end of her speech, she asked for questions. She was met with stony silence. This silence was not the result of a poorly developed vision, but of a failure to connect with the audience.

Consider this alternative. A leader needs to engage her organization in significant changes. Prior to talking to the organization, she thinks about how to create connection between herself and the group, between the group and her ideas, and between group members. She follows the advice in Chapter Three and widens the circle of involvement so that those who have information, authority, and responsibility, as well as those who will be affected by the proposed changes, will be present. She then does the following: Instead of meeting in an auditorium setting, with everyone lined up facing her, she sets the room up so that people can sit at round tables. Each table has an easel and flip chart. The meeting begins with people at the tables introducing themselves to each other and talking about why they have come to this meeting and their hopes and concerns about the proposed changes. The outcomes of these table discussions are posted on the easel sheets and shared table by table. Our leader then shares the reasons the changes are needed, and she outlines possible courses of action. The table groups then spend time discussing what they heard and identifying key questions. Again these are posted on the easel sheets and shared table by table. What follows is a lively question-and-answer session along with a discussion of the issues. At the close of the meeting, people are energized about future possibilities.

Even those who may not agree with the direction feel included in the change process and feel that their concerns are valid and understood—not because they've been manipulated into feeling good, but because they have been included and their concerns have been recognized.

In this example, the leader considered creating connection of equal importance to discussing the proposed changes. She created a room that made connection easier by using round tables and easel pads to record the discussion. She began the process by allowing time for connections to form between people at the tables. She then took time to connect at the level of purpose, finding out the hopes and concerns of the people in the room, and she gave those issues equal weight to her own. The leader did not give a long-winded one-way speech. She spoke briefly about her ideas and created time and space for those assembled to discuss them among themselves. She made sure that she was understood and created an atmosphere where she could respond to issues and concerns. Having done this, she then proceeded to discuss with the group the possibilities for the future. By paying attention to connection, the leader laid the foundation for deeply engaging the organization in the change process. Instead of being met by yawns, she created connection, interest, and excitement.

Building Connection

For many of us, connection appears to be a magical process, mercurial and capricious. We know and understand its importance, the ability to come together and achieve great outcomes, but we do not know how to produce these results on a consistent basis. Sometimes it happens and sometimes it does not. It does not have to be that way. In the remainder of this chapter I will discuss specific actions that leaders can take that connect people to each other:

- Creating a compelling purpose
- Honoring the past and present as you create the future
- Building relationships
- Connecting the parts of the system
- Creating opportunities to show people that their voice counts
- Making the whole system visible

Creating a Compelling Purpose

Why is purpose important, and how does creating a compelling purpose relate to connecting people to each other? Think back to the narratives about the hurricane and the connected business team, where a higher purpose brought people together and produced connection. Saving people's lives, helping those in need, and making a difference is what drew people together and allowed them to stay connected during difficult times.

In almost every organization I visit, people wonder why it is that they can work so effectively during a crisis and so ineffectively at other times. It is during times of crisis that purpose and meaning become crystal clear. When people connect with the purpose and meaning, they put self-interest aside and work for the common good.

Does this mean that you have to create organizational crisis in order to produce connection? No. I disagree with those who say the way to bring people together is to create a "burning platform." My experience is that change brought about by fear does not last. Once the fear is removed, people return to old habits and patterns. The burning platform—and the unity of purpose it inspires—soon turns to ashes.

Dr. Dean Ornish, author of *Reversing Heart Disease,* states that it is not the fear of another heart attack or bypass surgery that motivates people to make the necessary lifestyle changes that will prevent future cardiac events. Rather, it is the desire to feel good and to live a full life. The fear that is present for the first few weeks following a heart attack or bypass surgery dissipates as time passes and pain diminishes. Unless patients are able to replace their fear (the crisis) with a desire to improve their quality of life, it is not probable that they will be able to sustain the necessary lifestyle changes (such as dietary restrictions, smoking cessation, and exercise) over the long haul. In other words, they must find a higher purpose.

Many organizations go about identifying purpose by building what is often called "the business case for change." This case for change is designed to convince people that the organization must change and it must change now. Typically, the business case for change is extremely logical and thorough and organizations that use it believe that the sheer logic of the case for change will carry the day. While creating a case for change is a necessary first step in connecting people with purpose, on its own it can't create a purpose powerful enough to produce connection. For a purpose to connect people, it must reach both their heads and their hearts. In other words, they must perceive the purpose as meaningful. If the reason for change lies solely in the numbers and in the logic, it will not stir people's hearts. So there must also be a "case for meaning."

The case for meaning provides a way for organization members at all levels to attach personal meaning to the change process. For most people, a purpose of saving $30 million from a hospital budget does not have meaning. They may recognize the need, but it does not create energy or excitement. On the other hand, a purpose of improving health care so that doctors and nurses can care for people in the way they envisioned when they entered the profession has tremendous significance. Not long ago, a doctor talked with great emotion about his experience treating trauma patients in an emergency room. "The trauma cases became just pieces of meat to move along. I stopped seeing them as human beings. What we are proposing here—the organization's change strategy—will allow me to feel human again because I will be able to treat patients as human beings." He had found meaning.

Not long ago when my colleagues and I were working with a school district, the discussion turned to the reasons why changes needed to occur. As members of the team shared their personal reasons, they talked about the need to improve test scores, provide a better educational experience for students, and stimulate learning. These are the kinds of things that you would expect to hear from educators. As the discussion continued, we probed deeper and asked why it was important to achieve these goals. Suddenly, I noticed that one of the teachers had tears in her eyes. I asked her what was going on. She then proceeded to describe a recent incident in which a student was killed on his way home from school. This was not a gang member, not a kid who was in trouble all the time. This was a kid who liked school, who got good grades, who wanted to make a better life through education.

Through her tears, the teacher said, "This is more than improving test scores and creating a new curriculum. It's about saving kids. That's what we're about. We're about saving kids. That is the difference we have to make." Others in the group immediately grasped what she was saying. This realization about the meaning of their work produced a higher level of connection among the group members and increased their energy and desire to act.

Some words of caution: First, no written statement of purpose will engage people. Essential as it may be to write down a purpose, it is the dialogue *about* the purpose that engages people, that provides the opportunity to attach meaning. Plaques on the wall do not engage people. In far too many instances, such plaques serve only as silent testimony to failed change processes. Second, you cannot create meaning for others. People must be able to find meaning in the purpose for themselves. A purpose that is meaningful to you is not automatically meaningful to others. Finally, the way you go about creating a purpose is just as important as the purpose itself.

Honoring the Past and Present as You Create the Future

Why should we honor the past and present? After all isn't the future what it's all about?

Certainly, our flavor-of-the-month culture does not value events from the previous month. The newest change is always considered the best change, the one that will really make a difference. Previous initiatives were misguided, this one carries with it the truth.

The failure to link what you are doing today to what came before it creates confusion. People wonder if what they did before was wrong. Were their efforts for naught? Was all that time and energy just a waste of time? If what we did before was of little value, why will what we are doing today turn out differently? Why should I commit to a new action when I see yesterday's efforts thrown out like last night's garbage?

Today, many people who participated in the quality-improvement and employee-involvement efforts of the 1980s and 1990s are wondering what happened to these efforts. Subsequent change initiatives

HOW TO CREATE
A COMPELLING PURPOSE

Bring together a microcosm of the organization, representing different levels and functions. Talk to this group about the need for change and enlist their help. Together with them, co-create a compelling purpose, one that includes both the case for change and the case for meaning. Do not expect them to immediately validate your reasons for change. Expect them to push back. In fact, if they do not, beware. The output of this work should be a purpose that is deeper and more compelling than your original thoughts.

Creating a compelling purpose involves dealing with the following questions: What do we want to be different in the organization because of this change? What do we want to be different for ourselves because of working on this task? What is it about the purpose that has meaning and would be worth doing for us personally? The members of the group creating the purpose must be able to answer these questions for themselves.

Revisit your purpose. Rarely are groups able to create a compelling purpose on the first try. Deal with these questions a week later at increasing levels of depth. Let them rest and then come back again. Look at your purpose in the cold light of day. Does it have depth? Does it have meaning? Does it engage you? Does it engage others? Test your purpose with those whom you want to engage. What is their reaction? How do they respond? Revise and make changes to your proposal based on their reactions.

> Now you are ready to engage the organization. Remember—written statements of purpose never engage. Dialogue is what produces understanding, excitement, and engagement. That is why written vision statements never change anything. Bring people together and discuss the purpose with them. Listen to both their positive and negative reactions. Develop and deepen the purpose with them. The very process of creating the purpose together connects people to each other and to the purpose.

that build off the skills learned in earlier efforts fail to build the link and make the connection to the past. This leaves people feeling certain that their past efforts were not valued, and uncertain about the purpose and direction of the current change process.

History links us to those who have preceded us. It gives us a sense of place and roots us in our culture. To value history is to honor those people and actions that have preceded you. It says that what they did has value and meaning. Acting without a sense of history is operating in a vacuum. Ortega, the Spanish philosopher, says that if you do not know history, you are condemned to repeat the mistakes of the past. It is important to link what you want to create in the future to what you are doing today and what you plan to do tomorrow.

History is about telling stories. It is about passing down traditions. Storytelling informs the listener of the reasons why things came to be this way. Storytelling links the new initiates to the elders of the tribe. It produces connection between the storytellers and the listeners and between past actions and future actions.

An advertising agency that I know conducts storytelling days on a regular basis. In these sessions, the old-timers talk about the history of the firm, unusual client experiences, and the battles that were won and lost. It is through these stories that newer members of the organization begin to understand why things are the way they are. The norms and values of the organization are communicated through these storytelling sessions.

In *Leading Minds: An Anatomy of Leadership*, Howard Gardner states that organizations have stories about themselves: we get things done; we are customer oriented; we pull together in a crisis; we're smart, creative people; it's dog eat dog around here; we never implement anything; people in this organization are unreliable. Gardner goes on to state that organizational change is a process of shifting the story an organization has about itself. To shift the current story, you must first understand the story in place and how it came to be.

Honoring the past as we create the future produces connection because it provides links to both the people and the events that have preceded us. It provides a mechanism for valuing past efforts and building on them as we move to the future. It connects us to our shared organizational history.

Building Relationships

We don't have time for this relationship stuff. We've got a job to do here. Why do we have to spend our time worrying about relationships? What does building relationships have to do with the task before us? Everything.

Change does not occur in isolation. Communities of committed people produce organizational change. For a collection of individuals to create the coordinated sets of actions necessary to produce change, they must feel connected to each other. The community must know its members and be able to count on them for action. Trust, connection, and knowledge of the personal resources available within the community transform a collection of individuals into a community of people capable of producing coordinated sets of actions.

In *Ritual: Power, Healing and Community*, Malidoma Patrice Somé shares the following thoughts about community: "What one acknowledges in the formation of the community is the possibility of doing together what is impossible to do alone. . . . The community is where we draw the strength needed to effect changes inside of us. . . . What we need is to be able to come together with a constantly

HOW TO HONOR THE PAST AND PRESENT AS YOU CREATE THE FUTURE

Hold storytelling sessions. Have the elders of the organization pass on the folklore and let the new members tell their own stories. Let everyone say what brought them to this organization and what keeps them invested. Ask people to share stories about what they are personally proud of and what disappoints them about the organization. These stories build a shared database of common history and experience.

Create maps and links to the past. Show how previous efforts have contributed to where you are today. Make these links explicit. Honor previous efforts and contributions that allow you to move on to the next step.

Create learning histories, in-depth studies of previous change processes. It is through these histories that the organization learns what worked and what did not work about the change process so that it can build on its previous experiences.

Build in closure and renewal. Create processes through which you actually end a change effort. Do not just let it fade away. If it was a failure, do not allow it to twist slowly in the wind. Provide a proper ending, a session or retreat in which people can discuss what went wrong and learn from it. Renewal provides an opportunity to examine periodically what is working and what is not working. It is through renewal that change processes stay alive and well.

increasing mind set of wanting to do the right thing, not even knowing how or where to start." The "coming together" that Somé calls for starts with connection.

A business leader said recently, "What always amazes me is how much you learn when you spend a little time getting to know people. What rich experience there is! What resources are present! You learn about resources and talent that you would not have believed possible when you first sat down with this group of strangers. The whole human experience is laid out for you before your eyes if you just spend a little time listening to others." We—my colleagues and I, and the team from the organization—had just spent a little over an hour in small groups getting to know each other before proceeding with the business of the day. It started with the usual name and occupation. But then it went deeper. We talked about what brought us to this meeting, what our hopes and concerns were, our personal histories that made being here and working on this task important to us. It was through these conversations that we moved beyond being names, roles, and titles to become unique individuals who were building connections with each other.

Building relationships increases trust, and when trust increases, relationships are strengthened. This is a mutually reinforcing pattern. In learning more about you, I find places of connection. I find out that we have similar interests, or life experiences, or I learn that you have unique talents and abilities. The more I get to know about you, the more I trust you. When I trust you, I am more willing to work with you and take risks. As we work together we learn more about our strengths and weaknesses. If in the process of working together, I learn that you are reliable and that I can count on you for support, then trust increases still further and our relationship deepens.

The Future Search Conference is a process for working in large groups to create an organizational future. One of the activities in that conference has participants post on a wall their personal experiences over the last thirty years. It always astonishes me what goes up on the wall. People write about births, deaths, marriages, divorces, leaving home, returning home, struggles with alcohol and substance abuse, heart attacks, cancer. When you look at the wall, you see the whole range of human experience. And because the data is posted anonymously, no one knows whether it is the vice president who has a terminally ill child or the janitor who is suffering from cancer. When people see the personal struggles of everyone in the room, connection deepens, because for a brief moment they take off their organizational masks and let others see them as the complex human beings they are.

Shortly after having bypass surgery, I participated in such an exercise. I remember feeling particularly vulnerable and alone. I thought that I was the only person in the room who had had such an experience. I remember as I was about to write in the personal category—*bypass surgery, 1992*—I saw someone else had written *heart attack,* and another had written *stroke,* and another had written *cancer.* Suddenly I went from feeling alone and vulnerable to realizing that others in the room had had experiences similar to my own. We had not spoken and I did not know who they were, but I no longer felt alone in this group of people. A first connecting link had been formed.

Connecting the Parts of the System

The voice from the back of the room asks: *"Why do we have to work together? I know my job! If I do my job and everyone else does their job, then we will be fine. The people I work with every day—we know what to do. I just don't get why I need to be working with these other groups."*

The answer is that today's organizations are complex systems that require intricate coordination to be effective. Gone are the days when we could do our own thing and it was okay. Even simple mechanical systems such as cars require connection to be effective. If the electrical system is not connected to the engine, the car does not start. What differentiates organizations from mechanical systems is that their composite parts are human beings. It is the human element that makes organizations real, that enables them to think, to act, to produce goods and services. Because any organization is composed of people, it can be thought of as a system that has a mind. In *Mind and Nature,* Gregory Bateson states that systems that can be said to

HOW TO BUILD RELATIONSHIPS

Listen, listen, listen until you feel you cannot stand it anymore and then listen some more. Listening builds relationships. Listen with understanding and empathy. Work for understanding, not agreement.

Stand in the other's shoes. Try to understand the world from the other person's point of view. Imagine what it would be like to see the world from their perspective and based on their experiences.

Start your meetings with check-ins. Take time to get to know one another beyond names and titles. Talk about hopes and aspirations. Talk about fears and apprehensions. Discover the unique resources that each individual brings. Even if your group has been meeting for some time, take time to find out what is going on with each person. Listen to whatever is on their minds before you begin the meeting.

Allow time for depth. Many organizations begin their gatherings with introductions and activities known as icebreakers. But because the business leaders are in a hurry to get on with "real" business, these activities often lack depth, cutting short the time necessary to really break the ice.

Consequently, the meeting starts out on a shaky foundation. If the organization spent more time building relationships and connecting members with one another before starting work on the stated purpose of the meeting, people would build a solid foundation for that work and it would proceed more smoothly.

Additionally, connection occurs throughout a process, not just in the first five minutes. Having time to explore

> issues and develop relationships throughout the meeting is essential.
>
> Legitimize the personal. Create time and activities that support the expression of personal feelings. The personal is so illegitimate in today's business environment that you would have to go a long way before you crossed the boundaries of inappropriate disclosure.

have a mind have certain characteristics. One of these is that the parts communicate.

Organizations today are made up of a myriad of departments, functions, sales offices, branches, plants, warehouses, and other units. To effectively produce goods and services, these parts must communicate. Communication is the lifeblood of a living system. As information passes from one part of a living system to another, it enables the system to adapt to ever-changing conditions. This capacity to self-correct is a characteristic of all living systems.

For example, you are driving down the street and suddenly a child darts in front of your car. In an instant, information is transferred from your eyes to your brain. Your heart rate and blood pressure increase. Your skeletal system is brought into action as you slam on the brakes and the car screeches to a halt, stopping within a few feet of the frightened child. Because the parts of your human system were in communication, they were able to process crucial information and take corrective action.

As another example, a telephone company I worked with had a long-standing problem with directory assistance. It took three days from the time a person got a new telephone number until it appeared in the operators' database—so for three days, the operators were giving out incorrect telephone numbers. This problem was not new; in fact, it had been around for a long time. Each part of the system—hardware manufacturer, software developers, database managers, and directory assistance operators—were aware of the problem and each had tried to solve it. Unfortunately, these prior efforts had never involved all the component parts: the operators would work with the database managers, or the software people would work with the hardware people. Then, during a conference to redesign the directory-assistance function, all the relevant parts of the system were brought together. Because representatives from the hardware manufacturer, software developers, database managers, directory assistance operators, and customers were present, a solution developed within a couple of weeks. Now new numbers appear in the database within a matter of hours. In this scenario, all the relevant parts of the system were brought together to examine the issue, share information, and solve this long-standing problem.

Creating Opportunities to
Show People That Their Voice Counts

As a new employee for a public utility company, I naively filled out a questionnaire about the organization. I even filled in the spaces for comments, expecting something to change. Weeks and months passed by, and nothing happened. The questionnaire soon became a thing of the past. I never received any information about the results of the questionnaire, nor did the organization change. I learned very quickly that my voice did not count and I soon disengaged from the organization.

When people know their voice counts they become engaged. But what does it mean to know that your voice counts? It does not mean that you get your way every time. What it does mean is that you experience yourself as being heard, understood, and able to influence the change process. When this occurs, people become engaged. When it doesn't, people disengage.

Leaders always know that their voice counts. The power of their office assures that. They know that they can influence the course of the organization and make things happen. Knowing that their voice counts, people feel powerful and act decisively. When people experience

HOW TO CONNECT
THE PARTS OF THE SYSTEM

Once you have widened the circle of involvement to include the whole system, the following ideas will help you get the parts of the system talking to each other:

1. *Work in max-mix groups.* "Max-mix groups" is a phrase coined by Kathie Dannemiller, of Dannemiller-Tyson Associates, to describe groups that contain the maximum mixture of people present. Each of these groups is a microcosm of the whole. Each person present represents one of the stakeholder groups that are part of the system. These groups provide an opportunity for people from the various functions and departments to learn from one another. By including everyone's perspective, these groups develop a shared understanding of the issues.

2. *Work in stakeholder groups.* These groups contain people of like interests. They could represent departments, levels of the hierarchy, or issues and interests in the organization. These groups provide the opportunity to examine an issue from a particular point of view.

3. *Structure conversations within max-mix and stakeholder groups to develop understanding rather than agreement.* Conversations that produce understanding are based on deep listening, empathy, and the ability to put yourself in the other's shoes. Conversations based on developing agreement often take on a win-lose atmosphere. Listening for understanding produces connection between the parts, while listening for agreement produces division. Provide opportunities for people to share their work in which the goal is to understand what is being said, not to tear it down.

4. *Conduct walkthrus.* Walkthrus are a mechanism to connect those who have been directly involved in the change process with those who have not. The walkthru is a structured communication process that brings information from those who have been deeply involved in the change process to those on the periphery and then incorporates the information from those on the periphery to those directly involved. This process connects two key components of the change process.

5. *Face the issues, not each other.* Literally this means to arrange the chairs in such a way that people are facing statements of the issues. Use easels, large whiteboards, or a wall covered with butcher paper to record the elements of your discussion. When people face the issues, conflicts are reduced because everyone's energy is focused on the matter at hand, not on winning over the person who is sitting across the way.

their voice as not counting they feel powerless. They then band together and create collectives that give them a stronger voice (labor unions, political coalitions, special interest groups) or they withdraw. Today's organizations can no longer afford to have employees who disengage from the organization because they feel their voice does not count.

When asked to participate in change processes, people often say, "If they know what they want to do, why don't they just tell us? Don't ask our input if your mind is already made up." They do not want to be part of a process that is designed to make them *feel* as if their voice counts when in actuality it does not. Manipulative processes disengage organization members because they quickly learn that their voice does not count.

A consistent pattern that my colleagues and I notice with the Conference Model is that the number of people who volunteer to participate in the process increases as the process continues. We believe that this occurs because the conferences and walkthrus are designed so that everyone's voice counts. As people experience being listened to and understood, and as they see that their ideas are incorporated into the process, they become engaged and want to continue to participate. They also tell their friends about it. This results in an increasing number of people engaging in the change process as it continues. People want to be part of something in which they know that they can make a difference.

In their classic *HBR* article, "How to Choose a Leadership Pattern," Robert Tannenbaum and Warren Schmidt describe various leadership behaviors from simply informing people about a proposed change to involving them deeply in the change process. As people move along this continuum, they experience their voice as having more and more influence. Tannenbaum and Schmidt suggest that leadership behaviors that provide organization members a voice in the change process increase the quality of the decisions, improve teamwork, and increase motivation.

Making the Whole System Visible

When it comes to understanding the organizations in which we work, most of us understand best our own jobs and the work groups of which we are a part. Knowledge of the system in which people find themselves dissipates the further they go from their day-to-day work group. In my experience, most people are ignorant of the larger system in which they work. In fact, it is not uncommon for people to spend their entire career in one department or function. When problems arise, this unawareness of how things work in the larger system often leads to shortsighted and suboptimal solutions. Issues are resolved in favor of one workgroup, unit, or organizational silo, not for the good of the whole.

One organization I know conducted classes for customers on its manufacturing process. Its managers believed that having more knowledgeable customers would improve relationships. Because the

HOW TO MAKE SURE PEOPLE KNOW THEIR VOICE COUNTS

Provide opportunities for two-way conversations instead of one-way monologue. Work for understanding rather than agreement. Support those who may disagree with you and make sure that they experience being heard and understood. When someone presents an opposing view, ask who else feels this way. Encourage and invite disagreement and listen attentively to opposing points of view.

Create feedback mechanisms so that people can see what happened to their ideas and how they were included or the reasons why their ideas were excluded from the final outcome.

Employ *multi-voting processes*—that is, processes in which people are encouraged to vote for a series of choices. For example, give participants a number of adhesive dots and have them place their dots on the proposals or options of their choice. This process is useful for choosing between alternatives and for ranking priorities. The multi-voting process is a powerful way to let people know that their voice is equal to anyone else's in the room.

Co-create the future together. As previously discussed, many change processes involve people only at the implementation stages of the new strategy or direction. At this point the only voice people have is in saying how to make it work or why it won't work. By involving people in the change process from the very beginning, you are saying that they have a voice in more than implementation. They have a voice in shaping the future direction.

customers knew how the manufacturing process worked, they were able to interface more effectively with their counterparts in the manufacturing organization.

Unfortunately, people who worked within the organization were not afforded the same opportunity to learn about how the whole system worked. Some people had worked for twenty years in the same department. They were experts in their part of the system, but had little knowledge of what happened once work left their unit and proceeded through the rest of the manufacturing system. They understood in only the most rudimentary way the impact their actions had on the rest of the system—or the impact problems occurring in the rest of the system had on their own work. Because of the organization's failure to make the whole system visible they were ignorant of the system where many people had spent their whole working careers.

When the whole system is visible, a number of things occur. First, people experience themselves as part of a larger whole. They are no longer just a job or a role, but are connected to the whole system. Second, they see where they fit in the system, becoming oriented in time and organizational space. They understand how the work that precedes theirs enables them to do their job effectively, and how their job affects the work of those whose contribution comes next. Lastly, when people see where they fit, they are able to make connections with other people in different parts of the system. These connections or links smooth the flow of the work and enhance collaboration.

The Medical Insurance Story

Imagine for a moment that you are a major health care provider processing thousands of patient claims a month. Each claim has to be evaluated to determine if medically appropriate care has been delivered. Whenever a standard or practice changes, the physicians have to approve the changes and the legal department has to review them. All the rules governing how claims are approved or denied have to be

HOW TO MAKE THE
WHOLE SYSTEM VISIBLE

There are a variety of techniques and processes to make the whole system visible. The large group process called Simu-Real is based on making the whole system of interactions visible to all. In this process, people take on the functions and roles of either an existing or a proposed organization and examine the impact of their connections on each other as they work out an issue. As the activity goes on, people are able to discover how the system actually works because they are able to see and experience the system in action.

The Conference Model uses several activities to make the whole system visible. Sometimes we use ropes to demonstrate the connections between parts of the system. Each group is given several piles of rope and asked to link ropes to other groups with whom they have connections. When you do this with a large enough group, the ropes become a spiderweb of connections. People soon discover that some units have lots of ropes going back and forth and some groups have very few. Participants are asked to pull on the ropes that represent the most important interaction, or the most frequent communication. Between some groups, the tugs and pulls are very strong, between others they are very weak, and between others they are nonexistent. Sometimes tugs and pulls affect the whole system, pulling it in a certain direction. People also learn that when you let go of the ropes, you go nowhere. In short, the ropes make the system's interaction visible to all and produce a kinesthetic understanding of the connections that are present in the room.

Passing the Order Through is another activity that makes the whole system visible. In this activity, a person representing a product or service moves through the system. Chairs and tables in the room are arranged in such a way to represent various stages in the production or service delivery process. As the person stops at each station, the group identifies what they do to the product or service. In this way, people develop an understanding of how work flows, where duplication, redundancy, and waste occur, and where value is added. In this way, the whole system becomes visible.

Mind-mapping also makes a whole system visible. In this process, the group identifies all the trends that may be affecting the organization at this time. These trends are mapped on large butcher paper, and people sit facing the map as it is developed. When completed, this picture of the external environment helps to make the whole system visible.

reprogrammed in each one of the operating systems. Then training has to be provided for all the claims supervisors and examiners on how to use the new review policies. Making incorrect medical policy decisions creates problems with regulatory bodies, increases costs, and decreases member satisfaction. Creating and implementing a process to ensure the smooth and timely execution of medical policy changes is thus essential to the organization's success. How would you go about addressing the problem?

In the case I'm thinking of here, five attempts had already failed to design and implement a process that would enable medical policy changes to be embedded in the systems and used by the appropriate claims examiners. Learning from past mistakes, a new team composed of a physician, an organizational development consultant, and an ace project manager decided to use an approach that fully engaged the organization in the change process. Working with a planning group that represented a microcosm of the organization, they designed a large group conference including sixty participants from all the stakeholder groups, including physicians, attorneys, system programmers, claims supervisors, and examiners.

The large group sessions began by encouraging conversations in which participants could get to know each other. At table groups, they answered questions such as "Why did I come to this organization?" and "Why do I stay?" These conversations enabled people to connect to each other as people, not as functions that typically argue with each other on the phone. Many of these people had worked together for years but had never actually met. The energy in the room began to rise.

Next, the CEO spoke to the participants about why this effort was so critical to the organization, how it would affect customers, and how it could improve staff satisfaction. He spoke from his heart and he let them know how much he was counting on their wisdom and dedication.

Next, the group had a conversation about the current state of affairs. They used a map of the current process to show people the way the work was currently organized, where hand-offs and delays occurred, and where disconnects proliferated. This was eye-opening for everyone involved. The reactions ranged from "Yep, that is how it is" to boisterous laughter at the insanity. Then they spent time hearing from various customers of the process about their frustrations as well as their requirements for a successful process. Seeing the map and hearing from the customers had a profound impact on the participants. There was total commitment to redesigning the process and a shared sense of purpose for making the implementation successful. Now it was time to go to work.

The group came back together for the second day of the conference to draft the workflow for the desired state. With Post-it notes, flip chart paper, and markers they created a new approach to drafting and implementing new medical policies. All of the customers' and stakeholders' views were represented in the design, and the process was built around meeting customer requirements.

When participants reflected on their experience, they expressed satisfaction at their ability to have candid, nonblaming conversations. But most important, they expressed their willingness to be a part of the project after the conference and make the implementation a success. One physician participant reflected: "When we started, you had sixty people who came into the room hating each other, when we left, you had sixty people in the room who did not want to leave and volunteered to be a part of the implementation. I'd say the approach is working."

The truth was that the work so far had been successful, but the process had just begun. The project manager and subteam leaders created a detailed plan to implement the workflow changes that came out of the conference. There were organizational reporting relationship changes, technology and system changes, and behavioral and skill changes. Subproject teams were created using a mixture of conference participants and other stakeholders to execute the work detailed in the project plan. Leadership stayed engaged throughout the process.

Within six months, the organization saw demonstrable results. By the end of the first year, its people had reduced the process cycle time by 75 percent. They increased the number of policy changes made annually from 2 to 186. Finally, they achieved over 80 percent customer satisfaction with the outcomes of the process redesign. The redesign effort was successful because people were enabled to understand the issues that prevented them from meeting customer needs and to develop a shared sense of purpose for improving the way they worked together.

Summary

Connection builds trust and trust deepens connection. It is a critical element of the human condition often ignored in today's organizations. Connection is a function of head, heart, and hands.

Leaders can create the conditions under which connection can occur in many different ways. A compelling purpose has the power to connect people to each other and ideas. It is the foundation of any successful change process. Connection also occurs when you honor the past as you create the future, building bridges from what has occurred before to what you are about to create. Taking time to build relationships is critical to increasing trust and connection. Connection also occurs when you bring the various parts of the system together so that people from different parts of the organization can share ideas and experiences. Similarly, connection occurs when the whole system becomes visible and people come to understand how they fit in the larger scheme of things. Finally, connection occurs when people know that their voice counts, when they not only feel heard and understood but have the experience of making a real difference.

5

Creating Communities for Action

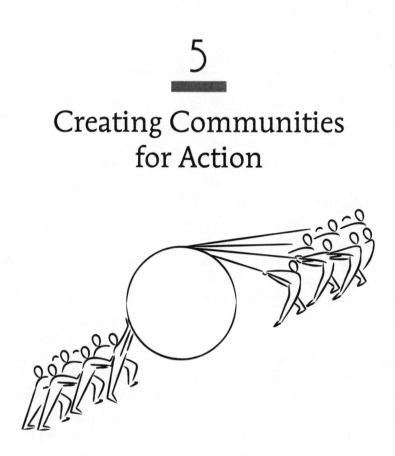

I nvolving people in the change process and helping them connect to each other is only the beginning. At this point, all you have is a larger group of people who may feel some connection to each other and the task before them. This chapter and the next identify the conditions by which people can, if they choose, move from a collection of individuals to a collaborative community of people who are willing to act. I am using the words *conditions* and *choose* intentionally, because the desire to become a community of people willing to act must come from within. Although leaders can foster conditions where community is possible, they cannot mandate community. Much like a farmer who grows a crop, the leader can till the soil, plant the seed, and provide irrigation, but cannot make the seed grow.

What Is Community? Why Is It Important?

I define a *community* as a group of people who willingly come together and put time and energy toward achieving a common goal or goals. The willingness of people to pool their talents and energy makes a community different from a typical business unit. In most business organizations, people work together because they know they must, not necessarily because they feel a sense of connection with others who want to achieve the same outcomes.

Meeting the demands of an increasingly complex environment creates enormous stresses and strains on individuals and organizations. Communities provide a place where people can draw on each other during these stressful times. Research on stress management indicates the importance of giving and receiving support, and communities provide this support during the inevitable stresses of any change process. When a person or group of people falters the community picks them up and helps them continue the journey.

There have been any number of times when my colleagues and I have become disillusioned during the course of a change process and received the needed support to carry on because we had been able to create a community of people who cared about the outcomes. I remember one time when we had a particularly bad day at one of our large group sessions. A discouraged group of consultants met with the company's planning group during the evening to review the plan for the next day. As consultants, we were ready to throw out the agenda for the next day and start over. However, a machine operator said, "Hold on, sometimes it just takes people awhile to get on board. I think we have a good plan for tomorrow and I think it will work. We've had this happen before and I think we'll be okay this time too." As he talked others joined in and agreed with him, and the more we listened, the more we realized he was right. So we stayed with the plan and the next day was extremely successful. Had we not had the support of this rich community of people, we would have changed the agenda and quite possibly have made a difficult situation even worse.

Dialogue provides the vehicle that allows community members to discover common ground. There may be things that they disagree about, but they also learn that there is a wide space of agreement within which they are able to take a coordinated set of actions.

Many change processes talk about the importance of having a champion to lead a change effort. But after a while, even the strongest champion gets weary. When you create a community of people who are connected to each other and the outcomes, many champions are born. Moreover, in much the same way that geese share the leadership of their formation over a long migration, a community of champions provides the resources for the long haul that successful change requires. Creating community creates champions.

Today many organizations are developing team-based structures because they believe that collaboration and teamwork are essential to meeting the demands of a rapidly changing environment. A closer look at these organizations finds that some groups are teams in name only while others are exemplars of teamwork and collaboration. What is the difference between these groups? I believe it lies in their members' abilities to develop a sense of community, to work together and put their wholehearted selves into achieving outcomes. Organizational structures can support effective teamwork, but they cannot produce people who care. Top-down leadership styles cannot produce community.

At this point, you may be saying, *"I understand the importance of community, but we are here to run a business. I am a business leader, not a community organizer. My goal is not to bring people together to sit around the campfire and sing 'Kumbahyah'!"* I agree with you that the goal is not to build campfires and conduct songfests. The goal is to produce an engaged organization, one that matches the following description:

▪ *People grasp the big picture,* fully understanding the dangers and opportunities.
▪ *There is urgency and energy* as people become aligned around a common purpose and create new directions.

- *Accountability is fully distributed throughout the organization* as people come to understand the whole system.
- *Collaboration across organizational boundaries increases* because people are connected to the issues and to each other.
- *Broad participation quickly identifies performance gaps and their solutions,* improving productivity and customer satisfaction.
- *Creativity is sparked* when people from all levels and functions, along with customers, suppliers, and important others, contribute their best ideas.
- *Capacity for future changes increases* as people develop the skills and processes to meet not just the current challenges but future challenges as well.

These benefits cannot be achieved through command-and-control behaviors, nor can they be achieved through organizational structures. When leaders try to achieve these results through such methods, they produce resistant and compliant organizations in which people do what is required and no more. No one can create high-capacity, collaborative, creative organizations through top-down, hierarchical processes.

The Community Dilemma

However, it does no good to simply tell leaders to give up traditional leadership behaviors and become community organizers. So how does a business leader foster community? In *The Careless Society,* John McKnight explores this question by comparing institutions to communities. He says that the structure of institutions exists to control people, and thereby to create predictable outcomes. The structure of associations (or communities) is the result of people's acting through consent. He goes on to say, "There are many goals that can only be fulfilled through consent and these are often goals that will be impossible to achieve through a production system designed to control."

Table 5-1 summarizes how McKnight compares the community or association with the institution.

Table 5-1 Consent Versus Command as an Organizing Principle

Community or Association	Institution
Based on the notion of fallibility—things can and do go wrong	There is an orderly perfection to things and institutions are designed to create that order
Inclusive rather than exclusive—there is room for people with differing ability	Only the ablest survive and dominate
Consensual contribution is a primary value	Contributions can be controlled and predicted
Responds quickly	Bureaucratic requirements slow response
Recognizes individual characteristics	Has great difficulty in recognizing individuals, values
Cares for people but has difficulty producing goods and services	Can provide goods and services but has difficulty caring for people
A place to express citizenship	Many rights of citizenship are forgone for employment
Nonhierarchical	Hierarchical

So here is the dilemma. Organizations by their very nature need predictable outcomes. We need the trains to run on time, airplanes to land safely at their designated locations, and the gizmo we purchase in the store to do what the salesperson said it would. On the other hand, we know that it takes people with the characteristics of the engaged organization to make these organizations work. Without people who care about the outcomes, organizations can never meet the goal of predictable outcomes. Caring is a function of consent, not of control. The question is, can these systems be embedded within each other? Is it possible to create communities in which action is based on consent within organizations that are designed to control people and outcomes? The answer is yes.

Comparing the previously identified characteristics of an engaged organization to McKnight's description of communities, it turns out that the two are natural partners. McKnight describes communities according to the following characteristics:

- Capacity, that is, the fullness of each member. The sum of each individual's capacity represents the power of the group.
- Collective effort. The essence of community is people working together.
- Informality. Expressed through relationships that are not managed.
- Stories. Stories and storytelling represent the way knowledge is acquired.
- Celebration. Communities are characterized by laughter and singing.
- Tragedy. People in the community have explicit knowledge of tragedy, death, and suffering.

These six elements manifest themselves in the engagement paradigm.

Capacity, the fullness of each member, is fundamental to the engagement paradigm. Moving from change processes that are controlled by the most powerful and the best and the brightest to include people from all levels of the organization, customers, suppliers, and other stakeholders makes a huge statement that everyone has the capacity to contribute to create a new future. Furthermore, when participation in the process becomes voluntary, you reinforce the idea that everyone has something to contribute. Even those who might be opposed to the change process, those who might be harmed by it, or those who will soon be retiring are welcome. When you widen the circle of involvement, you make room for everyone, their strengths as well as their weaknesses. You accept the fact that some will think faster or slower than others. You understand that some will write well while others will be better speakers, some will be conceptual while others will require concrete examples, that some will be very logical while others will wear their hearts on their sleeves. When you believe deeply in the idea of capacity, all are welcome.

Recently, as part of an effort to reform health care in England, the National Health Service designed processes based on the engagement paradigm to involve communities in improving their health care.

One of the topics was diabetes management. Where earlier conferences involved only health care providers—doctors, nurses, and nutritionists—this conference included patients aged five to eighty and their families. Many doubted the capacity of the young people to contribute, but their contribution led to one of the stunning outcomes of the conference. They had unique and essential information. It turned out that the schools were unintentionally adding to the problem. They hired "dinner ladies" whose job was to cook for the children and see that the food did not go to waste. The dinner ladies prepared meals that were harmful to diabetics—and then made sure that the children ate them. The children, who had received education about their disease, were trying to follow the advice of their doctors, but were powerless in the face of the dinner ladies. This conference resulted in developing a process for educating the dinner ladies on the nutritional requirements of diabetics and helping them to provide healthy food for children. This issue was not identified when health care professionals met with each other to address the issue of diabetes management. It was only discovered when young patients interacted with health care professionals. This interaction occurred because the planners believed in the capacity of everyone to contribute in both identifying issues and developing solutions.

Collective effort is the foundation of the engagement paradigm. When people connect to each other and to the task, they put collective energy toward achieving outcomes. A core concept of the engagement paradigm is that the changes facing organizations today require collective effort. Single individuals can no longer bring about the changes that are necessary in today's rapidly changing environment. What is required is a community that is ready and willing to act.

Barn raising is an interesting example of how a common task and collective effort build community. In barn raising, members of the community come together to help a neighbor build a barn. The community voluntarily assists their neighbor because they know that this task cannot be accomplished alone. As people work together to build the barn, the experience in turn strengthens their bonds of community.

Expressing informality in relationships that are not managed goes way beyond the informal dress code that is being adopted throughout the business world. Informal dress helps, but if the relationships do not shift along with the change in attire, then all we have done is bought comfortable wardrobes. Changing how we think about relationships is essential. The various methodologies whose principles are aligned with the engagement paradigm, including Future Search, the Search Conference, Participative Design, Open Space, Real Time Strategic Change, Whole Scale Change, and the Conference Model all subscribe to this principle. They provide frameworks where people can come together and create new futures, but do not prescribe what those futures are or control how people will interact with each other. The outcome is always in doubt. Will people choose to continue to fight the old fights they know so well, or will they choose a different way of working together? Open Space provides the least structure when it tells participants, decide the issues you want to work on, work with the people who share your interests, and if it is not working, find another group.

Stories provide the vehicle by which we learn. McKnight observes that universities come to know about things through studies, organizations come to know about things through reports, and people come to know about things through stories. Stories and storytelling are essential to the engagement paradigm. In Chapter Four, I talked about Gardner's concept of organizational stories. All organizations have stories about themselves—and an organization must change the story it has about itself if it is to change anything of importance. When organizations begin to work with the engagement paradigm, people find themselves telling stories. Whether told during "storytelling days" to include newcomers in a culture, or by people engaged in the Future Search Process describing their most proud and most sorry moments, or as part of the creation of an oral history during a Search Conference, stories do more than share knowledge, they create links between people. Storytelling is an ancient form of passing wisdom, the most ancient form of knowing.

An emergency room nurse told the following story during a conference to redesign patient care. "The patient came in with cardiac distress. Both he and his family were anxious because they had just learned of his condition. What he experienced was people running amok, procedures, consent forms, tests, the whole bit. No one attended to who he was or how he was feeling." Choking with tears, she said, "It still hurts today although it was a long time ago, because a few minutes later he coded and died. His whole experience with us was one of confusion and chaos. He died alone and afraid. The system's procedures are not more important than the patient."

Celebration expressed through laughter and singing is symbolic of community. Not long ago my colleagues and I were conducting a workshop in which teams from various organizations came together to develop change strategies based on the engagement paradigm. One evening, participants and faculty began to drift into the hotel bar. After a while a guitarist appeared. What followed was a two-hour songfest that included old favorites along with some old tunes with new lyrics designed to tell the story of the week's experience. We sat around the fireplace, sang songs, and joked about the week's events until the wee hours of the morning. As the saying goes, "A good time was had by all." The singing and laughter that occurred spontaneously was an expression of the community that had been built by four teams from four different companies who had been complete strangers to each other just a few days before.

Tragedy is openly shared in communities. It is not buried, not hidden. It is experienced and understood. Of late my colleagues and I were working with a paper mill to redesign the organization. During one of the large group sessions, we had people tell stories about their experiences in the mill, those things that they were proud about and those things that they were sorry about. A number of years before, there had been a serious accident in which two people lost their lives and a third was permanently disabled. At first people were reluctant to talk about it. In fact, the first person who spoke said, "Well there was the accident." Then another person mentioned "the accident." Finally, I asked what had happened. Reluctantly, people began telling the story, saying how hard it was to this day even to think about it, let alone talk about it. Others talked with great pain and anguish about the two funerals and their coworker who was never the same again. Some talked about the great teamwork that occurred when people risked their own lives trying to save the injured. Still others talked about how important it was to leave work with the same body parts you had when you started the day. Others talked about their own near misses and how lucky they were. Many recognized that they developed a new level of consciousness regarding safety because of this experience.

Not every organization experiences the profound tragedy that this organization did. However, other kinds of tragedies occur regularly in organizational life, and discussion of these tragedies is typically blocked and called illegitimate. Think about the victims of downsizing who are immediately escorted off the premises without an opportunity to say good-bye or to be offered good wishes by their coworkers. In the name of corporate security, both the people involved and their coworkers are prevented from expressing their feelings. No good-byes, no best wishes. Turn in your ID and company property, and out the door you go. Everyone carries deep wounds from experiences like these. When a community experiences tragedy but is unable to acknowledge that tragedy, it fractures. Fear, hurt, and distrust take over, breaking up whatever level of community previously existed. In the engagement paradigm, we honor the expression of tragedies that befall people in the course of organizational life. For out of these tragedies great learning often occurs.

Through the valuing of everyone's capacity, working together to achieve a common goal, and informality, the benefits of an engaged organization are achieved. Through the experiences of stories, celebrations, and tragedies, the engaged organization forges links with its members and produces learning within the system. So the question becomes not whether you can afford to have community within an organization, but whether you can afford not to have it.

The community dilemma has deep roots in our national history. Alexis de Tocqueville was a French count who came to the United States in the 1830s to try to understand the North American experience. A distinction that he immediately recognized between the United States and Europe was the existence in the United States of communities of citizens that came together to identify and resolve issues. He noted three distinct features of U.S. communities: First, they were groups of citizens who empowered themselves to decide what the problem was. Second, they empowered themselves to decide how to solve the problem. Finally, they often decided that they would become key actors in implementing the solution. Isn't this what leaders want? Organizations in which people take the initiative to identify and resolve issues. Isn't this what organization members want? The freedom to identify and resolve issues that affect them.

In his essay about the benefits of civic engagement, "Bowling Alone," Robert D. Putnam states that when we are engaged, we establish common ground and trust our neighbors. Because trust is established, we are able to work together effectively. What he is pointing out is the reciprocal nature of connection and community. When we develop connections with people, we trust them and because we trust them, we are willing to work in community with them. Similarly, the process of working together to achieve a common goal also produces trust. As we work together with others, we learn about them. Through this process, we learn to trust each other. We learn each other's strengths and weaknesses and, in the process of building something meaningful together, form new bonds.

Although the chapters in this book are presented sequentially, they represent this reciprocal relationship. Widening the circle of involvement includes more people in the process and widens people's perspective so that they can let go of self-interest. Connecting people to each other creates links between people and builds trust. Creating communities for action sets up conditions in which people care about the outcomes of what they do together. In addition, embracing democratic principles provides a set of norms and behaviors that governs people's actions and behaviors. However, all of these steps are interconnected and we work on them simultaneously. When we widen the circle of involvement, we employ democratic principles. While we are building connections between people, we are building community, and while we are building community, connections between people are created. As in any system, improving one aspect of the system benefits the other aspects.

Commitment

Commitment is one of the defining characteristics of a community that cares and is willing to act. To quote a line often attributed to Goethe, "Until one is committed, there is hesitancy, the chance to draw back, always ineffectiveness."

When people commit to a course of action, they are willing to hold themselves and others accountable. They are willing to put forth extraordinary amounts of time and energy to reach a common goal. Committed people make things happen. They are not ineffective, they are not hesitant, and they produce results. This is not a secret. Everyone knows that commitment is important, but what does it take to produce commitment?

Pathways to Commitment

My partner Emily Axelrod and I think about commitment as occurring in the mind, the heart, and the hands: commitment occurs as a result of being attracted to an idea (mind), because it fits our value system (heart), and because of the experience we have working together to produce an outcome (hands).

Logic-driven commitment occurs in the mind. Under these conditions, the facts in the situation cause me to become committed to a course of action. This can be the result of being influenced by newspaper articles, books, stories, television, or any other source of information. Logic-driven commitment results from an understanding of the facts. When organizations create the case for change, they produce a logic-driven document in which the facts are so overwhelming that everyone will commit to the proposed course of action. Sometimes this works. Statements of facts—market share is declining, customer service is abysmal, costs are out of line—can and do influence people. Unfortunately, it is not enough. I have seen leaders speak eloquently on the case for change, even accompanying their lecture with flashy slides, only to be met with yawns. Their belief that logic would win the day caused them to ignore the other two elements of commitment: the heart and the hands.

Commitment from the heart can start in one of two places. The first is through relationships. I become committed because an individual or group I know, respect, or admire asks me to become involved. I commit to action primarily because of my relationship with the individual or the group. The second is through personal values. If a change is consistent with my own values, then I am likely to commit to it. I become engaged because the course of action is in alignment with an important set of values that I hold. Examples include supporting Mothers Against Drunk Driving, improving public schools, working with youth, improving customer service, or being part of a high-performance organization. In this case, the alignment of values is driving my commitment.

In *Emotional Intelligence,* Daniel Goleman identifies the need to connect both the head and the heart. Goleman cites brain research that indicates that when we make decisions we employ two kinds of intelligence, a kind that deals with facts and logic, and a kind that deals with emotions and feelings. These two types of intelligence work together to produce good decisions and subsequent actions. The logical intelligence helps mediate the hot blood of emotions and helps us make rational choices. The emotional intelligence moderates the cold logic and is based on life experiences. When we say the decision feels right, we are applying our positive and negative life experiences to a set of facts and circumstances to aid in the decision-making process. Thus commitments based on logic alone lack an emotional grounding and commitments based on feelings alone lack an analytical grounding.

The mistake most leaders make when they seek to gain the commitment of others is employing only logic-based strategies. They mistakenly believe that once people know the facts they will commit to making the necessary changes. This view is only partly right. To produce commitment, both intelligences must be accessed.

Recently my colleagues and I were working with a manufacturing organization that was experiencing a great deal of difficulty: costs were out of line, market share was declining, and customers were dissatisfied. The leaders of the organization presented data to attest to these facts ad nauseam with little results. What they failed to realize was that at the value level, people wanted to be part of an organization that worked—one in which the current inefficiencies, rules that did not make sense, and waste and duplication were eliminated. The logical arguments about customers and market share never addressed these issues. It was not until the change process began to address the issues that did matter that people in the organization became engaged in the effort. Coincidentally and not surprisingly, there was a direct tie-in between these emotional issues and the logical issues of declining market share, cost, and customer satisfaction—but it took the emotional issues to make the logical ones come to life.

Hands-driven commitment is a result of personal experience. Initially, engagement may occur through my mind or my heart, but my hands actually sustain my commitment. By this, I mean that I might volunteer to be part of change process because it makes sense to me or because it fits my values. However, the experiences and interactions I have during the change process determine whether my commitment will deepen. If these interactions are positive, I am likely to deepen my commitment. Positive interactions can occur because of working relationships developed with other people on the project. Increased teamwork and camaraderie can occur as we work toward our goal and, consequently, deepen my commitment. Positive interactions also occur as we accomplish tasks and begin to see positive outcomes. Commitment deepens as people begin to see the results of their work.

People might volunteer to build houses for Habitat for Humanity because it makes sense to them or because it fits their value system. However, the important component is the experience of building the house. If the experience is enjoyable, and they feel like they are doing something worthwhile, their commitment to Habitat for Humanity will deepen.

An interesting result of the recent impeachment trial of President Clinton was the impact the trial had on the Senate. After the trial was over, no matter how they voted, the senators spoke about how the experience had deepened their commitment to the U.S. Constitution. They reported that as a group they had developed new bonds that would improve their working relationships in the future. This was a result of their experience of working together during the trial. It did not have to end up this way. The trial could have produced a divided body whose commitment to the U.S. Constitution, democracy, and to working together had decreased rather than increased.

The experiential component of commitment is extremely powerful. The experience of working together can increase the bonds of commitment or it can diminish or eliminate commitment.

Thus commitment occurs when we engage our head, heart, and hands. Put another way, commitment occurs when the mind, the emotions, and the experience come together and we say, This is something I will support with my time and energy.

Commitment Continuum

Many see commitment as a binary choice: someone is either committed or not committed. Another way to view commitment is as a continuum, reflecting degrees of commitment from passive to active engagement. As shown in Figure 5-1, there are five levels of commitment.

Consider the levels in detail:

1. *Not getting in the way.* This is a neutral form of commitment in which people will not oppose the course of action, but will not actively support it. At this level of commitment, people are silent but

Figure 5-1 The Five Levels of Commitment

Passive Engagement		Active Engagement		
Not getting in the way	Providing resources— no personal involvement	Personal participation	Taking a stand	Taking high personal risk

are carefully watching what is going on. As the change process continues, they may decide to increase their level of commitment.

2. *Providing resources without personal involvement.* At this level, people are willing to provide funds or share the credibility associated with their name, but they are not willing to do anything that requires any effort. A familiar example is giving money or your public support to a charity, but not personally participating in it. Organizational examples include providing the funding or the organizational time and resources for a change process.

3. *Personal participation.* At this level, you are willing to participate personally in the change. This means that you show up consistently and actively participate in the change process.

4. *Taking a stand.* At this level, you are willing to work actively to advocate for the change process and to involve others in the process. This also means speaking up when you see things are going wrong and actively working to make sure the process succeeds.

5. *Taking high personal risk.* This level involves more than taking a stand. It involves advocacy when you know that you have something personally at stake. This could include your career, the way others perceive you, or anything that puts you personally at risk because of your involvement.

This continuum is divided into two sectors: passive engagement and active engagement. Items one and two make up the passive engagement section, while items three, four, and five make up the active engagement section.

At least two factors can move people from passive to active engagement. The first is the perception that what is being proposed, the course of action, will result in substantive change taking place. People do not want to waste their time if nothing is going to happen. They also do not want to be part of a process in which the answers are predetermined. The second is the belief that their personal contribution and action will make a difference, that their active engagement will influence the outcome. People become actively engaged when they know that their voice counts. Conversely, if people are unable to see the possibility of results, or do not see themselves as being able to influence the outcome, then they will move from active engagement to passive engagement.

What Sustains Commitment

Sustained commitment involves five primary factors:

- *Positive results.* Seeing positive results from your efforts makes you willing to commit more energy and resources. Commitment increases when efforts produce results.
- *Information sharing and feedback.* Information sharing and feedback are mechanisms by which people can measure the effectiveness of their efforts. They allow people to learn about both the positive and negative consequences of their efforts, which in turn renews their commitment.
- *Support of others.* Knowing that others are involved and committed to the goals provides a form of social support. When individual commitment falters, others involved in the effort can bolster those who are losing faith. Their ability to see progress can renew and support others.
- *Increasing personal involvement.* Sitting on the fence does not sustain commitment. When people involve themselves more fully, they are likely to increase their level of commitment. It is also true that increased involvement sometimes causes people to lessen their commitment, if they learn that their voice does not count or that they do not agree with the purpose and outcomes. However, it is clear that increased involvement has at least the potential for increased commitment, while sitting on the fence has no effect whatsoever.
- *Walking the talk.* The more the actions of those who are supporting the change are congruent with what is being proposed, the more likely it is that others will want to become committed. If members of Mothers Against Drunk Driving are alcoholics who drive, it is unlikely they will be able to influence others to commit to action. Similarly, managers who want employees to provide input

and ideas but ask for them only after the major course of action has been chosen are less likely to create commitment than managers who involve everyone from the very beginning.

How the Engagement Paradigm Supports Commitment

The engagement paradigm has the potential to increase the level of commitment as people move from passive to active engagement. This does not always happen, but it happens more often than not. In addition to the five primary factors, the following six conditions contribute to increasing commitment:

- *Task.* The task has to be meaningful. It must have enough breadth and depth to engage people. The task must be compelling from a logical standpoint, a personal standpoint, or both.
- *Self.* People must see the possibility of a place for themselves in the task. Possibilities include assistance in creating the future, influencing outcomes, or implementing the proposed course of action.
- *Boundaries and ground rules.* There needs to be a clear set of boundaries that frame the purpose. When the purpose is clear, individuals can make informed choices about their level of commitment. Ground rules let people know where they stand. Having a clear set of ground rules about how people can participate and influence the change process encourages individuals to make responsible choices.
- *There is no one right answer—there are many answers.* The more substantively people are involved in dealing with issues, identifying courses of action, and implementing change, the more likely they are to increase their level of commitment. The more fully they participate in the planning, decision making, and implementing processes, the more committed they will be. This level of involvement will inevitably produce several solutions. In choosing a course of action, the depth of commitment is as important as the ultimate outcome.
- *The wisdom is in the room.* The people who are brought together to deal with the issues currently facing an organization actually live with these issues on a daily basis. Therefore, their inherent wisdom

needs to be trusted and valued. The answers are everywhere and in all of us. When you engage people at all levels and functions with key outside stakeholders, you are making a powerful statement about your trust and belief in their ability to create strategies and courses of action to deal with complex issues. Reichhold Chemical Company recognized this when it adopted the phrase "the solution is here" for its change process.

■ *Connection occurs before commitment.* Even though individuals can become committed either through logic or through the heart, I believe that it is when people feel personally connected that they commit. This is why I believe that it is so important to connect people to each other and to the task.

This last point bears restating. Talking with colleagues about meaningful change invigorates people and they learn from each other. When they are not connected, they are less likely to commit to a change. One of the issues in the United States today is our lack of connection, which makes it difficult for individuals and communities to come together and commit to action.

How to Foster Communities for Action

Desiring community and building it are two different matters. The presence or absence of a strong community can seem whimsical, a matter of fate, but there are three specific actions that can be relied upon to create the conditions under which communities are ready and willing to act. These actions are co-creating the future, understanding the whole system, and creating a learning environment.

Co-Creating the Future

Co-creating the future involves two important concepts: co-creation and maintaining a future focus. Building something together is very different from implementing someone else's ideas. It is also very different from brainstorming possible solutions and then turning them over to someone else to implement. When people build something together, they own it, it is theirs.

In their classic *Harvard Business Review* article, "How to Choose a Leadership Pattern," Robert Tannenbaum and Warren Schmidt describe four leadership styles and their relationship to employee ownership and commitment:

- *Telling.* The leader tells organization members what the change will be, how it will work, and how to implement it.
- *Selling.* The leader sells the organization on the merits of the plan. You know you are in a selling mode when leaders talk about gaining buy-in. For there to be a seller, there must be a buyer. In this case, the leader sells and seeks to get employees to buy.
- *Consulting.* The leader seeks input before making the final decision. The decision-making authority rests with the leader, but the organization members' ideas are sought and taken into consideration.
- *Collaborating.* The leader places all the facts on the table and calls upon organization members to work together to develop the solutions to the issue at hand.

When leaders work in the collaborative mode, they establish the conditions that have the highest probability for producing communities that are willing to act. The act of building something together creates a community of people who become committed to a course of action.

It is obvious that the telling and selling leadership styles do not produce commitment, but it is not obvious that the consulting style fails as well. With the consultative approach, the leader gathers ideas and opinions, then makes the final decision. Joint problem solving and decision making do not occur. This often leaves organization members frustrated because they never know for sure how much influence they have had on the process. The change management paradigm tries to blend a consultative and collaborative approach. There is high collaboration within its steering committees and design groups, but the committees' actions with the rest of the organization resemble a consultative approach. Those working within the change management paradigm often feel confused when the organization does not support their proposals because they see themselves as operating in a highly collaborative manner. What they fail to recognize is that much of their own enthusiasm for the change process comes from their ability to influence the outcomes. Creating communities that care and are willing to act requires more than just asking for information and ideas.

A classic example of this is the Detroit Edison experience cited in Chapters One and Two. The supply-chain improvement process had relied on people giving input to a steering committee and to various subcommittees. This resulted in the steering committee initially feeling highly motivated and having a high degree of ownership for the process. However, in the rest of the organization, there was little interest and ownership, despite the steering committee's hard work. When the steering committee decided to move to a collaborative style of operation and began to implement the principles of the engagement paradigm, ownership in and commitment to the supply-chain improvement process began to shift.

The second element is maintaining a future focus. *A future orientation stimulates action.* Have you ever noticed that when you are about to make a change in your life you notice that change everywhere? If you are about to buy a new house, the world seems full of "For Sale" signs. If you are about to buy a new car, you suddenly begin to see new cars everywhere. If you are thinking of having a baby, you begin to see babies and pregnant women everywhere. What is going on here? In our minds, we have a picture of the future we want to create. Suddenly our brains let in information that has always been there but we were unable to see. This new information shows up as possibilities, and we are motivated to take action. We know the future we want to create, see the possibilities, and act.

Ron Lippitt researched groups and found that when people discussed problems they actually got depressed about trying to fix them. However, when they identified a positive future they wanted to create, they became energized. In *The Path of Least Resistance for Managers*, Robert Fritz states that when people know the future they want to create and understand their current reality, structural tension is created. He goes on to state that when structural tension exists—that is, when there is a difference between the current state and the desired future—people resolve that tension by moving toward the desired future. In other words, a future orientation creates action.

Maintaining a future orientation does not mean that you ignore the past. Remember the importance of honoring the past as you create the future. You need to decide what parts of the past you want to bring with you as you create a new future and what parts of the past need to be left behind. But if you only reminisce about the past, you will create fond memories, not action.

Not long ago a hospital decided to redesign its patient care process using the Conference Model. Doctors, nurses, administrators, insurance providers, and patients came together to improve the patient experience. As the conferences progressed, many ideas were discussed and the picture of a more patient-oriented, compassionate hospital began to take shape. Following one of the conferences, a group of nurses took it upon themselves to offer patients hot towels at least once during their shift. The hospital of the future that was being created in the conferences compelled them to take an immediate step in that direction.

The change management paradigm has not always employed a future orientation, and when it has, it has not done it well. Quality-circle efforts and employee-involvement processes largely ignored creating a future and relied on a problem-solving approach. This often produced negative energy rather than creating engaging possibilities.

When the change management paradigm sought to incorporate the concept of vision, its attempts were woefully inadequate. Typically, visions were created by senior leaders and therefore lacked the richness that occurs when people with differing viewpoints and perspectives come together to create a vision. Having created a vision, leaders then faced the problem of selling people on their concept. The lack of involvement in the early stages of creating a future created unnecessary resistance as the vision was rolled out to the organization. Often the whole visioning process was reduced to endless wordsmithing, sloganeering, and plaques on the wall. The potential for creating an engaged organization based on an engaging future never materialized.

The importance of a future orientation is also contained in the liturgy of the Jewish High Holy Days.

> If some messenger were to come to us with the offer that death should be overthrown, but with the one inseparable condition that birth would also cease; if the existing generation were given the chance to live for ever, but on the clear understanding that never again would there be a child, or first love, never again new persons with new hopes, new ideas, new achievements; ourselves for always and never any others—could the answer be in doubt?

Would you trade everlasting life for a life without a future?

To summarize, the first of the two important elements of co-creating the future together is to involve a critical mass of people in the change process from the very beginning. Invite people to identify and clarify the purpose and help shape boundaries and direction. Together identify the future you want to create for the organization. In doing so, operate as partners in the change process, not as bosses and subordinates. The second is to maintain a future focus. In doing so, you create positive energy and see possibilities you were unable to see before.

Understanding the Whole System

Critical to the success of the community is its ability to understand the total environmental context in which it is operating. In *Future Search,* Weisbord and Janoff integrate the work of social scientists Solomon Asch, Eric Trist, Fred Emery, and biologist Ludwig von Bertalanffy, and identify key conditions for understanding the whole. They also state that when people understand the whole system they are operating in, they are able to let go of parochial self-interest and develop strategies for the common good.

These are the conditions they have identified:

- The relationships among the external environmental factors outside the organization or system under consideration
- The relationships within the organization or system under consideration

- The impact of external trends on the organization or system
- How the organization or system can work to improve its internal environment so that it can respond effectively to the external trends

From a practical standpoint, this means that you must widen the circle of involvement to include customers, suppliers, community members, and important others in order to really understand the issues in the external environment that are having an impact on the organization. The organization then works to understand the current interactions and relationships within the organization and the impact of these external trends on the organization. Finally, the organization must decide what it is going to do differently so that it can respond more effectively to the external environment. These four steps—understanding the external environment, understanding the internal environment, identifying how the organization currently operates in relation to the external environment, and determining how it can more effectively respond to these trends—are crucial to understanding the whole system and taking action.

The ability to understand the environment in which they operate provides people with the knowledge and insights they need to act. This understanding cannot be spoon-fed. It occurs when people are actively engaged in the discovery process. One of the activities in the Conference Model is called "passing the order through." As mentioned in Chapter Four, in this activity, a person pretends to be an order for a product or service and is passed through the system. The "order" starts with the customer and goes all the way to product or service delivery. Along the way, the different departments or functions identify what happens to that product or service. Soon the whole complexity of the system becomes alive and people discover the redundancies, duplications, and disconnects in the current system. It is through this discovery process that people develop an understanding of the whole system. When that understanding occurs, they cannot help but act.

A few years ago my colleagues and I worked with a chemical company that was using the engagement paradigm. The company's managers widened the circle of involvement in their change process to include a local environmental group. At one point in the conference, a representative of the environmental group spoke eloquently about the need to clean up the local river. Her message was that most of the pollution in the river came from individual actions, not corporate polluters, and that if everyone took responsibility for the river, it could be a place where their grandchildren could fish and swim. After hearing her message, when the organization identified the essential values for the future, a clean environment was one of the top ten.

This would not have been possible if this "outside troublemaker" had not been present at the conference. As the conference progressed, the relationship between the organization and its customers, suppliers, community, and environment came into sharper focus. People stopped looking inside and looked at the bigger picture. Customers and suppliers offered up ideas and actions for helping the organization become more competitive and reduce costs. None of this would have been possible if the organization had taken only an internal focus.

A common fear of those contemplating use of the engagement paradigm is that the process will deteriorate and produce unproductive conflict. That simply doesn't happen. Including the whole system, establishing human connections, and maintaining a future focus prevent this collapse into blame. Kathleen Madigan, a consultant and participant in one of our workshops, reports the following experience when working with a hospital on two different occasions. In the first occasion, only hospital employees and doctors attended the large group session. Soon everyone's worst fears materialized, blame was everywhere, among doctors, nurses, and administrators. Although everyone tried to look at external factors, they did so with their "internal eyes." On the second occasion, they invited important outsiders including insurance providers, employers, and patients—and blame disappeared. They heard the outside perspective directly and came to learn and understand the external trends bearing on the organization. Together they were then able to address what they needed to do to respond effectively to these changing conditions.

Creating a Learning Environment

I have seen repeatedly that as people come to understand the issues that are affecting them, they experience both depression and excitement. They become depressed about the complexity of the issues facing them, wondering how they will ever deal effectively with them, and then become excited about the possibilities for doing things differently that emerge in the process. Creating a learning environment means allowing all of these feelings to exist simultaneously.

A learning environment equalizes power. When people join in the spirit of inquiry and learning, everyone is empowered. As people learn and discover together, they begin to feel smart about the issues facing them. When people feel smart, they act smart, taking control of situations and problems and developing creative solutions.

Finally, a learning environment produces action. When people feel powerful, believe they understand the issues, and are acting smart, they want to deal with the issues that are affecting them.

Why Other Paradigms Do Not Produce Communities Ready to Act

Consider for a moment how the top-down and change management paradigms deal with the issue of creating communities that are ready and willing to act. Neither paradigm produces communities that are ready to take action, because neither is willing to make the necessary investments to sufficiently engage people. In the top-down paradigm, leaders develop the change strategy and attempt to sell their approach to the organization without having involved or consulted those who will be affected by the change process. And leaders employing the change management paradigm involve a select few to develop plans and strategies for others to implement.

In both these approaches, someone creates something for someone else to implement. Thus, both fail to engage the organization in co-creating the future. Today many organizations are struggling with the fact that they have difficulty implementing change processes.

What they fail to recognize is that co-creation produces commitment and that commitment rarely occurs when you are asked to implement someone else's plan.

The Berkeley Story

Imagine a city fire station that is larger than a football field. On the floor of the fire station is a 50'×75' map of the city with streets and buildings outlined in chalk indicating the new locations of city departments and divisions. This was the setting for a unique event in which the City of Berkeley, in California, sought to anticipate the impact of renovations at Berkeley's Civic Center building, home to about a third of the workforce. Every city department was affected. Staff was about to be relocated to a dozen different sites, mostly in the downtown area but some several miles away. Apprehension and uncertainty were rampant as organization members worried about how the city would coordinate functions internally and continue to meet the service demands of the community.

At one point in the "Fire Station Event," some participants were asked to move their chairs to their new office locations on the map on the floor. Others acted as citizens, each with a customer service need that involved multiple departments. As the entire organization observed itself, it became apparent that a typical citizen could easily become confused and even irritated when trying to navigate in the new system. It also became obvious that different departments with shared responsibility for performing a particular work process or meeting a service demand had very different ideas about priorities, customer service values, and public accountability.

Soon, self-managed breakout groups composed of mixed staff from different departments met and developed innovative ideas to help ease the transition and maintain good public service. A surprising realization that came out of this session was that not all of the breakdowns noted were due to the big move. Many of the existing problems were deeply rooted in the organization's standard processes.

The "Fire Station Event" was part of a major new initiative aimed at improving the timeliness, coordination, and effectiveness of service delivery to the Berkeley community. The initiative, called "Neighborhood Services," is premised on the fundamental belief that the city can do a better job in meeting the needs of the citizenry without necessarily increasing overall funding and resources. More important, it is based on the notion that the way to create a high-performing government organization and a healthy community is through participation and engagement within the organization and between the organization and the community. To accomplish these goals, Berkeley is using the engagement paradigm. A team of city employees attended the Association for Quality and Participation's School for Managing where my partner and I led a workshop on the engagement paradigm. At the workshop, the team decided that these principles would form the cornerstone of their initiative.

While some workers and members of the community acknowledge that the city government has performed well in specific areas, it has also been characterized as slow, expensive, overly bureaucratic, and providing lackluster services. Tellingly, whenever the city does perform well, it is usually in the face of a real or imagined crisis, and requires a cross-organizational team working together with some direct connection and dialogue with members of the community. Therefore, one of the goals of the "Neighborhood Services" initiative was to develop an organization in which this type of behavior was the norm, not the exception.

As the organization continues to engage in defining itself, planning efforts will address the need to bring voices and engagement from other quarters. The current plan is to involve a diverse group of employees including gardeners, street and sanitation workers, public health nurses, refuse workers, police officers, and firefighters, as well as nonemployees such as elected and appointed officials, citizens, and others. Community-wide events are planned, featuring living-room-level meetings to introduce the concept of Neighborhood Services, and with a stated purpose of looking for ideas on how the concept can be developed into a model that meets needs of neighborhoods. Other external events will include meetings with civic associations such as the Chamber of Commerce and the Rotary Club, as well as with large neighborhood-oriented associations such as the Neighborhood Network and the Council of Neighborhood Associations.

In doing this work, the Berkeley team hopes to change the nature of the conversations within government and between government and citizens, connect people in new and exciting ways, promote clarification of interdependent relationships, and create an understanding of the whole. They believe that, in doing so, they will have a more enduring and meaningful impact on the organization's and the community's capacity to embrace change.

Summary

Creating a community of people who have the energy, commitment, and will to implement needed changes within organizations that are predicated on predictability and control is no small task. Yet it is exactly the task that needs to be done.

On the face of it, the requirements of community inclusivity, acceptance of fallibility, recognition of differences, and consensual contribution seem to fly in the face of an organization's need for predictability and control. Commitment is an essential component of community—but it is not a binary choice. Rather it is a continuum of behaviors ranging from passive acceptance to active involvement. Creating communities for action begins when we widen the circle of involvement and connect people to each other and to ideas, and builds momentum as the community co-creates the future together, develops an understanding of the whole system in which the community finds itself, and forges a learning environment among its members. In the next chapter I will show how the final step, embracing democratic principles, provides the spirit that makes things happen.

6

Embracing Democratic Principles

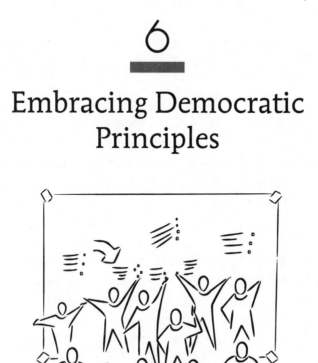

This is the hard part. The success of the engagement paradigm rests on the ability of leaders at all levels to embrace the democratic principles of equity and fairness, maximum sharing of information, open decision-making processes, and freedom and autonomy. Without these principles, it is possible to widen the circle of involvement, connect people to each other, and even create communities for action and still end up with a change process that fails. Because it lacks internal congruence, its leaders end up doing the right things for the wrong reasons—to manage resistance rather than create an engaged organization that both honors and profits from resistance. When such incongruity occurs, it will touch the wounds of previous manipulations and betrayals. Recognizing that the real goal of the process is to mollify them rather than to engage them fully in the change process, people will withdraw and disengage.

Learning from Change Management's Mistakes

Despite the best intentions of those who have used the change management paradigm, its processes typically have produced resentment and cynicism instead of an engaged organization. I believe that its failure is due in good measure to the lack of democratic principles at its core. Its advocacy of decision making by a select few "best and brightest" reveals that its foundational principles are not democratic but oligarchic. While Plato promoted oligarchy—government by the elite—in his great work, the *Republic,* the American soul was forged in the fire of democracy. When the outer trappings of a change process appear to invite participation but the implicit goal is to get people to implement the ideas of a small group of managers and consultants, people resist. When democratic principles are used only within decision-making groups while the practices of the formal organization remain hierarchical, people revolt through foot-dragging sabotage.

In moving to the engagement paradigm, it is important to learn from the past. By embracing democratic principles, you will prevent the incongruency that occurs with the change management paradigm. Additionally, the practices outlined in Chapters Three, Four, and Five provide for the creation of a critical mass of people who can sustain a change process in the face of the norms of the formal organization.

Why Embracing Democratic Principles Matters

I do not underestimate what is required to embrace democratic principles. For most leaders, this is a formidable task. Nevertheless, operating according to democratic principles is precisely what makes the difference between a follow-the-rules, resistance-prone organization and an organization in which people grasp the issues and initiate action.

At this point, you might be thinking, *Wait a minute here! Organizations are not democracies! The leaders of the organization are not elected representatives. If the engagement paradigm requires us to vote on everything or act like elected officials, I do not want any part of it.* I agree with you. Voting on every issue, even if it were possible, would bring organizations to their knees. And organizations are not democratic governments; in fact, they are not governments at all. They are concerns created to produce goods and services. With the necessary capital and means of production, the owner of the concern creates a system for producing the organization's product or service. Employees receive a wage in return for their labor, which either creates, enhances, or delivers the product or service. This is the basic employment contract. A fair day's work for a fair day's pay. The owner provides a place to work and as a result has the final decision-making authority. Employees are not citizens of the company for which they happen to work.

However, consider for a moment authoritarian forms of government. What is the first thing that a dictatorship does? It controls and limits information through state-run newspapers, television, and radio. Second, it makes decisions in secret so that the public is not able to observe how and why decisions are made. Third, it eliminates the rights of people to influence the direction of the country through voting. Finally, it denies the right of assembly, the right to come together and discuss the issues. People do not trust such a government to look out for their best interests, but they learn to keep their opinions to themselves as they do not trust their neighbors either. They drag their feet and do as little as possible to get along. As East European workers used to say, "As long as they pretend to pay us, we will pretend to work." Few organizations today are run as dictatorships, but many have remnants of authoritarian behavior. In these organizations, information is limited, decision making is a private affair, the ability to influence decisions is restricted, and people rarely convene to discuss issues that are of importance to the organization. Consequently, trust in the leaders decreases, commitment wanes, and creativity dries up.

Again, I am not suggesting that we run our organizations as pure democracies. Yet certain democratic principles can make a huge difference in organizations, helping to build trust, create commitment, and increase creativity. These democratic principles include equity and fairness, sharing information, public decision making, and increased involvement in the decision-making process. These principles are so deeply ingrained in the American culture that we take them for granted. In parts of the world where these freedoms are not in place, people willingly give their lives to secure them.

Leaders have long recognized that even though they may have the ultimate decision-making power, dogmatic approaches to organizational change do not sufficiently engage the organization to produce desired outcomes. They therefore frequently experience tension between opening up every organizational decision to the total organization and placing the decision-making process solely in the hands of the leadership.

The real question is, Under what conditions and circumstances does it make sense to deeply involve people in the processes of the organizations? The Vroom-Yetton leadership model provides the answer. This model identifies the conditions under which it makes sense for leaders to deeply involve organization members in the decision-making process and the conditions in which it makes sense to make unilateral decisions. Vroom and Yetton identify two critical components: the quality of the decision and the acceptance of the decision. Quality has to do with the correctness of the decision and acceptance has to do with the support necessary to implement the decision. Simply put, their research indicates that if the quality of the decision is certain and if acceptance of the solution is not an issue, then leaders are safe in following decision-making processes that are unilateral in nature. However, if there is more than one right answer and acceptance of the solution by organization members is not certain, then high-involvement processes are in order.

Vroom goes on to state that if leaders followed this model they would become simultaneously more autocratic and more participative! They would make more decisions on their own when conditions warranted, and they would also involve people more often in the decision-making process. Vroom goes on to state that leaders are more likely to err on the side of protecting the quality or rationality of the decision than they are to err on the side of overinvolvement. Decisions made by leaders are more likely to be ineffective because of lack of acceptance than because of lack of quality.

Unfortunately, this error is reinforced by current change management practices. In an attempt to protect decision quality, change processes are designed so that relatively few people make decisions about direction and strategy. Then, belatedly recognizing that acceptance is important, the process is opened up to more people when it comes time for implementation. People are involved after all the crucial decisions have been made, when it no longer matters, when it is too late for meaningful involvement. The current change management paradigm creates a Solomon's choice by splitting quality and acceptance. What is needed is a holistic solution. Creating and implementing high-quality change strategies requires high involvement from the very beginning.

In change management processes, there may be an egalitarian spirit among the members of the parallel organization, and their committees may even operate in a way that ensures equity and fairness among the members. They may share information with each other and experience a great deal of freedom and autonomy. However, for those outside the parallel organization, not much has changed. They do not experience themselves as having a voice, they do not have adequate information, and their lack of inclusion in the process creates suspicion. Many leaders do not recognize the distinction between what may occur within the inner workings of the parallel organization and how the rest of the organization experiences the change process. They are often puzzled and disappointed with their failure to engage the organization in crucial change initiatives using what they believe to be highly participatory processes. In far too many instances, they give up altogether. The problem does not rest solely with their techniques but with their failure to truly and wholeheartedly embrace democratic principles.

What do I mean by "wholeheartedly"? Again I would like to cite the work of Dr. Dean Ornish on reversing heart disease. In addition to observing that fear does not motivate people to achieve lasting change, Dr. Ornish has observed that half-measures do not work. Not surprisingly, then, Dr. Ornish's approach requires much more of the participant than traditional approaches. The conventional treatment for heart disease as espoused by the American Heart Association suggests reducing dietary fat to approximately 30 percent, reducing cholesterol intake, and engaging in moderate exercise. What Dr. Ornish has found is that most people who follow this regime actually get worse instead of better! He suggests reducing total dietary fat to 10 percent, adopting a plant-based diet, engaging in moderate exercise, practicing stress management (yoga or meditation), and obtaining emotional support. Dr. Ornish's research shows that when people adopt this regimen, they are able to reduce coronary symptoms and increase blood flow through the coronary arteries, thus reversing heart disease.

The American Heart Association's response to Dr. Ornish's approach is that it is too radical. They say that although it may have merit, it is too hard to follow. So they recommend a process that appears easier but is known to produce frustration and failure. Many people start the AHA diet with the intention of improving their health. When they do not see the necessary results, they give up out of a sense of frustration.

I believe there is an interesting parallel between what happens when organizations dabble at the edges of democratic principles and what happens when people follow half-measures for treating heart disease. In both instances, people start out with good intentions and follow what is considered good practice. But because these practices do not go far enough, after a while, people become discouraged by their lack of progress and give up on the process altogether.

There is one more thing to be learned from Dr. Ornish's approach to change: *expect immediate success*. Dr. Ornish reports that people start feeling better shortly after they begin to adopt his regimen. When leaders embrace democratic principles, people experience the difference from authoritarian approaches immediately and want to continue.

You might find it curious to be spending so much time talking about heart disease in a book about organizational change. I have personally experienced Dr. Ornish's approach to lifestyle changes and in the process have learned more about change than in all my earlier years of consulting. Since 1981, when I was diagnosed with high cholesterol, I have attempted to modify my lifestyle so as to lower my cholesterol. In the beginning, I followed the American Heart Association guidelines for change with little success. In 1992, I had triple bypass surgery. Since that time I have been following Dr. Ornish's program. I incorporated his dietary guidelines and added exercise, stress management, and emotional support to my life. My cholesterol has dropped from the high two hundreds to one hundred eighty. More important, I feel better and am in better shape than at any time since 1981. Like others in Dr. Ornish's research, when I followed the easier program of the AHA, I got worse. It was only when I stopped doing half-measures and adopted the complete regimen that I began to experience real improvement in my health. Therefore, I believe that half-measures that make people feel comfortable but do not challenge them to make real change are doomed to failure. Organizations that compromise on democratic principles produce frustration and resentment for everyone.

The Democratic Dilemma

We've come a long way from the feudal systems in which lords owned not only the land but also the means of production, including the people who worked the fields. Today many of us live in societies founded on democratic principles. The ideals of equity and fairness, open decision making, and freedom and autonomy are universal in their appeal. Indeed, most leaders today recognize that authoritarian approaches to change do not work over the long run. Clearly, you can get someone to change through force, threat, or manipulation. But leaders know that this change in behavior will disappear once the force, threat, or manipulation is withdrawn. Thus most leaders today want to follow democratic principles. But doing so raises issues of predictability, power and authority, and fear. I call this constellation of issues the democratic dilemma. (See Table 6-1.)

Table 6-1 Democratic Dilemma

Issue	Leader-Centered Approaches	Democratic Approaches
Predictability	If I make the decision, I know the outcome.	If I involve others, the outcome is less predictable.
Power and Authority	If I keep decision-making authority then I have the power to make things happen.	If I include others in the decision, then I must influence and be influenceable.
Fear	If I decide, I have nothing to fear but my own abilities.	If others decide, I give them the power to harm both me and the institution.

Who will care for the whole? If a strong central leadership does not look out for the whole system, will the system break apart? Who will provide focus? If the leadership does not provide focus, where will it come from? Who will pull everything together? If there is no central leadership, will the system fall apart at the seams? Is *Lord of the Flies* the alternative? Without a parent, will the children destroy each other?

The horns of the democratic dilemma can also be thought of as two opposing belief systems. The first belief is that the leader and those the leader chooses are the only ones capable of determining the appropriate course of action. The second belief is that everyone in the organization is capable of determining the appropriate course of action. The democratic principles outlined in the remainder of this chapter are based on this second belief. These principles and behaviors provide a powerful set of guidelines for leaders who choose to embrace democratic principles.

Equity and Fairness

Equity and fairness means working together in a way that blurs the privileges associated with roles and titles. It means everyone has an equal responsibility for contributing to the outcome. It means that, when making decisions, everyone has an equal voice. It means everyone has an equal opportunity to participate in the change process to the extent he or she desires. Equity and fairness means considering the impact of change on everyone and developing evenhanded outcomes. Ultimately, equity and fairness also means that the rules of the game apply to everyone. Change processes that are designed to change lower levels of the organization while the top remains unchanged are built on unstable foundations and ultimately collapse.

An egalitarian spirit is at the heart of this principle. It is based on the notion that all of us have ideas, and all of us can contribute. It says that ideas and insight are not the sole province of experts and hierarchy. The fact that you are a member of the executive team does not make your insights more profound or your reasoning more correct. By the same token, those who are at lower levels of the organization also do not necessarily have special insight. Rather, the answers are everywhere and in all of us. Egalitarian spirit recognizes experts as having an answer, but not the only answer. And it says that all of us are experts.

The Directory Assistance Story

Awhile back, my colleagues and I were working with the directory-assistance function of a telephone company using the Conference Model to implement self-directed work teams. The planning group was struggling with the issue of how to involve as many operators as possible in the change process without affecting customer service. The leadership thought the best thing to do was to hold the large group sessions on the weekend. In the middle of the deliberations, one of the operators questioned why the company was going to spend the money required to pay everyone overtime on the weekend. She thought that they could better meet the goals of high involvement and maintaining customer service by holding the large group sessions during the week.

The large group sessions were held during the week with the following results. A maximum number of operators were able to attend the conference. Customer service for those three days was higher than normal. This increase was because those unable to attend put forth extra effort, recognizing the importance of what was occurring at the conference and the organization did not have to pay overtime dollars or cause the employees the inconvenience of coming to weekend sessions.

Fairness and equity engages people because it says that everyone's ideas and contribution are important. It says that all of us have an equal chance to be involved, heard, and to make decisions.

The Jury System: Fairness and Equity in Action

Fairness and equity is the basis of the U.S. jury system. We trust that a random group of people can deal with complex legal issues and determine guilt or innocence. Like any system, our jury system has flaws, but despite errors, our trust in the system remain intact. If we can trust the very foundation of law and order in our society to this system, why can't we bring that same spirit to the workplace?

Here is a radical proposition: What if we chose those who are to be involved in change processes in the same way we choose people to be on juries? Everyone in the organization would be eligible to participate in the change effort. The various constituencies or stakeholder groups would be given slots, and people would be selected from various constituency pools to fill those slots. It would be an obligation of everyone in the organization to participate in the various change initiatives that occur during the course of organizational life. In this way, those determining new change strategies would represent a cross-section of the organization. They would represent not only the various levels of the hierarchy, but also the various levels of interest in the process. A random selection process would ensure that all points of view would be represented in the process—not just those who were predisposed to go along or those who might benefit, but everyone.

At the heart of this proposition is the concept that organizational change is part of everyone's job. A right and duty of corporate citizenship, if you will. Everyone knows that it is the right and obligation of all U.S. citizens to serve on juries. Citizens who end up on juries take that responsibility very seriously: the power to take away someone's freedom or inflict financial penalties is not taken lightly. I believe that if everyone knew that at some point in their organizational career they would be involved in shaping the course of the organization, three things would happen. First, people would become better informed about the issues facing the organization. Second, power would be distributed throughout the organization, and a single constituency would no longer control change processes. Finally, because all employees would know that they would be on both sides of the change equation—sometimes as developer and sometimes as a recipient—people would take the obligation very seriously and consider not just the changes that were needed but the impact of those changes on everyone in the organization.

Evening Out the Results of a Change

Besides bringing people together in a way that blurs the privileges associated with roles and titles, as in the jury system, fairness and equity means considering the impact of the change strategy on those who will benefit and on those who will not benefit. It requires us to develop a just approach to working with both groups of people.

Recently a change process that involved downsizing from fourteen senior leadership positions to seven senior leadership positions took this novel approach. They asked all fourteen leaders to assume that they would be one of the persons whose job would be eliminated and to determine how they would like to be treated if that were to happen. What they came up with was striking in is simplicity. It called for the following:

- Each person should have a conversation with his or her boss as soon as possible. That conversation would begin with the person's finding out whether they had a job in the new organization.
- If the answer were yes, they would then go on to talk about the job and the roles, responsibilities, and expectations that came with that position.

■ If the answer were no, the person would be given feedback about the decision and then told whether or not other jobs were available in the organization or whether they would have to look for other employment. The boss would help the affected leader develop a strategy for looking for a new position inside or outside the company. Training and other assistance would be offered.

The results of this process were that some leaders ended up retiring and others took on different jobs within the organization. Some stayed at their same level and others took jobs at lower levels. However, everyone felt that they had been treated in a fair and equitable manner during the process.

In another change process in which downsizing was also inevitable, procedures for retraining and outplacement were developed prior to the start of the change process and shared with everyone. Even though people did not like the downsizing process, they felt that the process for dealing with those who would be worse off as a result of the change was fair and reasonable. As a result, during the change process, many people offered up ideas and strategies that suggested the elimination of their jobs! I believe this unusual behavior was made possible because people perceived the process to be fair and equitable and felt secure about how they would be treated if their jobs were eliminated.

When we employ the principle of equity and fairness, we balance the power in organizations. We do not completely eliminate hierarchy, but we level the playing field and allow more people to participate. The principle of equity and fairness looks at power as an unlimited resource—something to be shared and distributed throughout the organization rather than hoarded and controlled.

Maximum Sharing of Information

Recently one of our clients came up with the phrase, "Information is only of value when it is shared." Certainly, the widespread sharing of information on the World Wide Web supports this view, which

HOW TO PROMOTE EQUITY AND FAIRNESS

Open up the change process to volunteers. Identify the number of people you would like to include in the change process. Within this group, identify the various stakeholder groups or constituencies that are present within the group. Then decide how many people from each stakeholder group will be involved in the process. Then ask people to volunteer to participate based on their stakeholder group. If you have more volunteers than slots, use a lottery system to determine who will actually get to participate. This process eliminates the idea that management is just picking those who are likely to agree with them to determine organizational changes. If you are feeling adventuresome, try incorporating the jury process outlined earlier in the chapter.

Use round tables and sit in circles—or get rid of tables altogether. Most seating arrangements at organizational meetings and conferences emphasize hierarchy. People are either all lined up in rows to get the word from the authority or are seated at long tables where the head is clearly defined. Both of these processes limit human interaction. The circle is the natural way for people to interact. Changing the seating arrangements promotes democratic interaction.

Take experts off the pedestal. Include experts in your deliberations, but do not give them the last word. Have them join you at your round tables. Provide opportunities for interaction and dialogue. Treat everyone as an expert.

Consider the consequences of your change process. If it is possible that some people will be negatively affected, develop a fair and equitable process for working with them. Follow the golden rule: think about yourself in the same situation. How would you like to be treated? When change processes are fair and equitable, even those who might be negatively affected are able to participate. If the change process is not fair and equitable, then distrust abounds.

Apply the change process to everyone; do not exempt any level or group of people. If the purpose of the change is to increase teamwork, apply this purpose to all functions and levels. If you only reengineer the bottom of the organization and exempt the executives, the reengineering process is destined for failure. Change processes in which one group of people says that the other group must change are inherently inequitable. Apply the change process to the total system.

runs contrary to the view that information is a scarce resource and must be hoarded, that its power is diffused when shared. Shared information can influence. It can change opinion. It can cause us to reconsider plans. When information is not public, it is of little use except to manipulate others.

Senior managers often wonder why the rest of the organization does not see things the way they do. Often it is because senior management has information that has not been made available to the rest of the organization. Is it any wonder that decisions appear to be capricious when some of us have information that others don't? Information is what connects living systems. Without the information that flows through our nerves, we would not be able to live. The same is true in organizations. Information lets the organization know what is happening in both the external and internal environments. Equipped with this information, the organization can make appropriate decisions. Without this information, the organization is flying blind. Information, not lines on organization charts, is what links the system.

Leaders who attempt to share information often find it a frustrating process. They feel as if they keep sharing the same data over and over again, but no one is paying attention. In *Leading Change,* Kotter states that organizations during change processes undercommunicate by a factor of ten! What Kotter means is that saying something once does not ensure that the message was even heard, let alone understood. People often discount or deny data that indicates the need for change. As long as people are in denial, the information will not get through. What is required to help people work through their initial shock is repetition and depth. The message must be given through a variety of methods and with increasing levels of depth. There must also be time for interaction and dialogue so that people can absorb the meaning of this information.

In my experience, the methods leaders use to share information are lamentably inadequate. The expectation is that the information will be assimilated the first time it is shared. Typically information sharing is seen as a one-way process. Information is posted on bulletin boards and shared through company Web sites, newsletters, videos, e-mail messages, or speeches by leaders. What is missing from these approaches is discussion and dialogue. Maximum sharing of information is more than the mere passing of information. It requires two things: sharing information through a variety of channels and media, and the opportunity to discuss the issues with the leadership. Because everyone does not incorporate information in the same way and because people work through their denial at different rates, multiple opportunities and methodologies for information sharing and dialogue are required. This can include print and electronic information, one-to-one conversations with peers and supervisors, discussions at business meetings, and large group sessions to explore the issues from various points of view. Information sharing is not a one-time event, nor is it ever accomplished through one medium.

Sharing information is sharing power. We have power over others when some of us have information and others do not. You cannot have an empowered organization without a free flow of information. Unless people have information, they cannot make free and informed choices. Holding information creates dependency, while sharing information creates initiative.

Recently a group of nurses learned during a large group conference that it was taking them an average of eight minutes to respond to a patient's call. This fact and other information about the causes of this problem prompted them to take decisive action. Following the large group conference, the nurses met on their own and developed processes and procedures to rectify the problem. Within a month, these nurses had reduced the average time to respond to a patient's call to one minute!

In another organization, employees receive information about the financial status of the business on a regular basis. They understand the organization's costs, their competitors' costs, and what is going on in the world market. This produces interesting behavior on the part of employees at all levels. What you see is everyone—not just leaders—raising questions about the financial impact of organizational decisions. Because everyone has the same information, everyone is vigilant about how the company spends its money. Without maximum sharing of information, this would not be possible.

When information is public, individuals are able to analyze the information and make their own decisions. They are able to examine the facts of the situation and come to their own conclusions. They are not dependent on the analysis and interpretations of others. Public information is the cornerstone of independent thought and action.

Recently a change process required budget reductions. So that everyone could participate equally in the process, all the budget information was shared with the participants, including how the various line items were developed and the historical and comparative analyses of the data. The organization provided training to people who did not understand budgets and how they worked. This process allowed people to understand the basis for needed cost reductions and to determine potential opportunities. Maximum sharing of information was a necessary step that contributed to the organization's meeting both the financial targets and service requirements of the needed changes.

Sharing information builds trust; indeed, low-trust environments are characterized by the withholding of information. When everyone has the same data, everyone can contribute to the decision-making process.

Open Decision-Making Processes

Open decision making is the most difficult of the democratic principles to follow. The principles of equity and fairness and information sharing provide the foundation and context for open decision-making processes, but don't ensure that they will occur. This principle deals with the depth and breadth organization members have in shaping the future of their organization. When people are involved in organizational decision making, they have a voice. When leaders incorporate this principle, they share power and authority. Those who have followed this principle have described it as an exercise in "letting go without abdicating," meaning that it is important for leaders to let go of long-standing prerogatives while at the same time maintaining their knowledge, insights, and responsibility to the outcome.

There are three dimensions to democratic decision making: the extent to which it is unrestricted, the extent to which it is public, and the extent to which everyone can participate in the actual decisions.

Openness deals with how accessible the decision-making process is to other people. Unilateral decisions are not open to others, but when we widen the circle of involvement, we open the decision-making process to include others. Two features of the Conference Model support openness. The first is the large group sessions in which people come together to make decisions about the organization's future. The second is the walkthru process where those who were not able to participate in the large group sessions are able to contribute their thoughts and ideas to the change process.

HOW TO MAXIMIZE
INFORMATION SHARING

Think about what you consider confidential or need-to-know information. Does it really need to be confidential or shared on a need-to-know basis or is this restriction just a way to maintain power?

• Use multimedia and multiple channels of communication. Share information early and often.
• Remember that communication is a two-way process.
• Do not assume that because you say something it is heard or understood.
• Provide opportunities for dialogue.
• Spend one-third of the time in meetings sharing information, and two-thirds of the time discussing it.
• During meetings and large group sessions, make all the information visible. Use flip charts, easels, and large sheets of paper on the walls.
• Keep all the information public and available so that everyone has easy access to it.
• Prepare data packs of information so that everyone has the necessary background to participate on an equal footing.
• If people need special training (in budgeting or other skills) to understand the information, provide it so that everyone in the room can operate on an equal footing.
• Use processes such as walkthrus as information channels with the rest of the organization. The walkthru process provides the organization with a mechanism for sharing and receiving information. Supplement the process with written materials, videos, internal Web sites, and so on.

But it is not enough to make the decision-making process more accessible: it must actually be made public. When decision-making processes are public, they are transparent, witnessed by all. They are able to stand the light of day. There are no closed-door sessions. When people can observe the decision-making process, they come to their own conclusions about its efficacy. Trust increases as people witness the decision-making process.

But even making decision-making processes public is not enough. High-involvement decision making is not a spectator sport. To fully engage people, the decision-making process must also have room for their input. Kurt Lewin's research on leadership and participation supports this position. During World War II, Lewin worked with anthropologist Margaret Mead to identify ways of reducing consumption of rationed foods. In one instance, an expert lectured housewives on the need for changing their buying habits. In another instance the housewives were given the facts and time to discuss the issues, after which they made decisions as a group. The results are not surprising. People in groups that reached consensus through discussion changed their buying habits more than those in groups that received expert information through lecture. In consensus groups, the decision-making process was open, it was public, and it included everyone's input. Lewin identified a simple but telling principle: *We are likely to modify our own behavior when we participate in problem analysis and solution and likely to carry out decisions we have helped make.* In other words, high involvement in the decision-making process from the very beginning engages us in implementing the outcomes.

My colleagues and I are often called upon to conduct large group sessions to create organizational visions. A common occurrence is that the leaders of the organization have already created a vision and want to sell it to the rest of the organization. Frequently we are able to prevail on the leadership not to sell their vision but enter into a creative process with the organization to develop a vision for the future using the principles of the engagement paradigm. When leaders do this, they are often surprised by how close the vision that is developed by a wide spectrum of employees is to the one management had been hoping to sell. In many instances, it is even better—for everyone involved, managers, employees, and other stakeholders as well. This occurs because, as in the groups in Lewin's research, the people who attend the large group session participate in analyzing the data and collectively determine future actions. Because it is their vision, not one that was sold to them by the leadership, people become engaged in making that vision a reality. It is one thing for leaders to have a vision of a customer-oriented organization. It is another thing for a critical mass of people to want to create a customer-oriented organization.

In a printing organization, a pressman attended a visioning conference in which one of the elements of the organization's vision was becoming customer-oriented. After the session, he returned to work and realized that a critical set of proofs would not be delivered to a customer on time. Recognizing the importance of customer service, he personally delivered the proofs so as to meet a critical deadline. He did this without outside prompting because he understood the importance of customer service as a result of his participation in creating the organization's vision for the future.

As much as I advocate involvement in decision making, I do not see it as a panacea to every organizational issue. The Vroom-Yetton leadership model and Tannenbaum and Schmidt's model of leadership provide guidance. Simply put, leaders can open up the decision-making process as they move along a continuum from telling to selling to consultative to fully participative processes. Leaders can use less democratic processes the more they believe that there is only one right answer and that people will go along with the proposed solution. The more there is a possibility of more than one right answer and the more that they will need the organization's support to implement the solutions, then the more they need to involve people in the process. When it is necessary to have high levels of involvement, then the democratic principles outlined in this chapter provide the critical elements for success.

Freedom and Autonomy

Freedom and autonomy are essential democratic principles. When people are engaged, they cannot help but act. Restricting freedom and autonomy diminishes action. The tension that occurs with this principle

HOW TO CREATE HIGH-INVOLVEMENT DECISION-MAKING PROCESSES

Widen the circle of involvement, provide people with the information, and involve them deeply in the decision-making process.

Clarify ground rules and boundaries. Identify clearly what is open for discussion and what is not open for discussion. It is better to have a narrow focus than to involve people in a decision process and then tell them that they have exceeded their decision-making authority.

Identify the rules ahead of time. For this decision, are you just looking for input? Or have you already identified alternatives and now are asking people to determine which alternative is best? Is it a decision where you will participate jointly with a group of people and are willing to live with the outcome? Is it a decision in which you are delegating authority and, as long as the group meets certain boundary criteria, you will support any course of action? Again, people need to know and understand the rules of the game. There is nothing worse than to think that you were participating in a joint process only to find out that the answer was predetermined and you were supposed to somehow come up with this predetermined answer.

Use processes such as consensus building and multi-voting to determine outcomes. Consensus building means listening and including various viewpoints to determine options. It means creating situations in which people experience their voice as counting and in which understanding is as important as agreement. Multi-voting is important because it demonstrates that everyone has an equal voice in the outcome.

is that the freedom and autonomy must be in service of the larger whole. Fears of chaos abound when leaders picture everyone in the organization doing their own thing. However, they also recognize that if organizations are to respond to rapidly changing conditions, they cannot cling to bureaucratic structures that ensure predictability while limiting freedom and autonomy. The trick is to provide enough freedom and autonomy so that people can respond to changing conditions, but not so much that chaos reigns. It is a problem that is similar to that faced by those of us who live in free societies: How do we balance individual freedom with the rights and needs of the whole society?

Freedom and autonomy occur frequently within the engagement paradigm. When people volunteer to be part of the change process, they are expressing both their freedom and their autonomy. Their participation is not dependent on their supervisor's approval. Everyone in the organization has an equal opportunity to participate in the process. Within large group sessions, people experience freedom and autonomy in a number of ways, when they exercise their right to vote on proposals and initiatives, when they volunteer to be part of follow-up committees, and when they speak out and discuss different points of view. Even when people choose not to participate, they are exercising freedom and autonomy.

For some leaders, the concept of freedom and autonomy is difficult. In one organization that I worked with, the leadership wanted to create follow-up committees to the large group session they held. The leaders felt that they would support nine such groups. They arrived at this number because they felt they could provide guidance to (translate as "keep control over") these groups. The conference was more successful than anyone hoped for and there was sufficient energy and enthusiasm to create twenty follow-up teams. The prospect of having so many teams "doing their own thing" in the organization frightened the leadership and they did not sanction all the activities of these twenty teams. An engaged group quickly became disillusioned and disengaged. Contrast this with another organization that also predicted that it would have nine follow-up teams. When there was sufficient interest and energy to create twenty-three teams, the leadership saw this as an indicator of the success of their efforts and moved quickly to develop processes to encourage and support this level of engagement.

Frederick Emery, the eminent social scientist, was a strong proponent of creating organizations in which freedom and autonomy are present. Emery's belief was that for organizations to respond effectively to rapidly changing conditions, people must have the freedom and autonomy to act. This could only occur when jobs within the organization met certain characteristics:

- Variety and challenge
- Elbowroom for decision making
- Feedback and learning
- Mutual support and respect
- Wholeness and meaning
- Room to grow

You can provide freedom and autonomy within the engagement paradigm and ultimately within the organization itself by applying these criteria to the change process.

Leadership Behaviors That Support Democratic Principles

The democratic principles described in this chapter become reality when leaders start behaving differently. The principles provide a guide to action, but it is the leader's behavior that makes the difference. I am putting the responsibility for this shift in behavior directly on leaders because they are the ones with the legitimate organizational power and they must make the first move. It is not that I believe that they are the only ones who must change; rather, given the way things currently are, they must make the first move and they must sustain the process. They must also withstand the pull of the organization for them to act in more traditional ways that sabotage democratic principles. Additionally, success requires everyone in the organization

HOW TO CREATE
FREEDOM AND AUTONOMY

- *Provide variety and challenge.* Engaging people in critical organizational change processes provides them with challenging experiences outside their normal job activities. They are exposed to different people, ideas, problems, and decision-making processes.

- *Provide elbowroom for decision making.* Creating room within the change process for people to make decisions on their own creates the needed elbowroom. The process must allow for input and participation in developing the future. When people can look at a strategy or decision and say that they helped to shape it, they develop a sense of pride in the decision and work to implement it.

- *Provide feedback and learning.* Create situations in which people can learn from each other during the change process. Create "mutual feedback groups" in which one group presents their proposals to another group and receives feedback. Then reverse the process. Not only do the ideas get better, but also both groups learn in the process. Create situations in which people can learn about the organization, the environment in which it finds itself, how the organization is currently responding to changing conditions, and how other organizations have responded to similar situations. This is the learning organization in action.

- *Build in mutual support and respect.* Treating all ideas as valid and all people as having worth goes a long way to create mutual support and respect. When we incorporate the equity and fairness principle, we create mutual support and respect.

> • *Choose topics that have wholeness and meaning.* This means engaging people in processes that have value and meaning for both them and the organization. Do not waste engagement on trivial pursuits.
>
> • *Leave room to grow.* This means providing the opportunity for people to show that they can do more than their narrow job descriptions. Do not limit your sense of what is possible by the current job that someone holds. Provide opportunities for people to do more and you will be surprised by the outcomes.

to shift to new behavior patterns and live by these democratic principles. This means that organization members must move beyond dependent relationships with leaders and engage their own freedom.

What are the leadership behaviors that make a difference?

- *Listen, listen, listen, and then listen some more.* Listening creates understanding, builds rapport, and creates trust. The heart of democratic action is respect for opposing points of view. When leaders listen, they do more than show respect for the other. They implicitly share power by saying that the other person's point of view is of equal value to their own. When leaders do not listen to opposing points of view, they are saying there is only one person whose voice counts—mine.

- *Create a safe enough environment.* This means inviting dissent. It is important that leaders make it okay for people to state opposing or controversial points of view. This, combined with listening for understanding, creates safety. How people with opposing points of view are treated determines the safety of the environment. Everyone watches how they are treated and calibrates their actions based on these events. If the environment is unsafe, vital ideas and opinions go underground. If the environment is safe, then ideas come forward and creativity is sparked.

- *Bet on self-management.* This means do not do for people what they can do for themselves. Bet on Emery's principles. Create conditions where they are possible and watch people flourish. Change your role from controlling outcomes to creating conditions under which self-management can occur.
- *Stay with uncertainty.* Do not abandon the process at the first moment of fear and uncertainty. Do not fall back to what is safe and sure. Stay with the uncertainty of the moment. Support these principles in the midst of chaos, confusion, and even conflict. In fact, this is when you need to listen more than ever before, when creating a safe-enough environment is crucial, and when you must not hedge your bet on self-management.

Recently, near the end of a large group session whose purpose was to design a new organization, a leader was confronted with a situation that put her faith in democratic principles to the test. Her behavior in this situation demonstrated to everyone her commitment to these ideals. Prior to this incident it looked as if we were going to develop a creative organizational design and finish on time. Then an issue developed that could not be resolved before the scheduled end of the session. The various points of view were so different that it became apparent that more time was needed. There were some who thought that the process ought to halt while a committee made up of various representatives decided the issue. Others thought the leader should make the decision. The leader did not succumb to either of these alternatives. She said the group had come this far together and would finish together. She reconvened the group two weeks later and within a matter of hours, the issues were resolved. A new organizational design emerged that had the support of the conference participants. What was needed was more time rather than arbitrary action. The leader listened, created a safe enough environment where differing views could be expressed, stayed with uncertainty, and bet on self-management. Her behavior demonstrated more than any formal statement her commitment to the engagement paradigm and its underlying principles.

The Washington Alliance
for Better Schools Story

Consider for a moment how the Washington Alliance for Better Schools, a nonprofit consortium of eleven school districts in and around the city of Seattle, incorporated the principles for successful engagement into developing schools and programs that prepare students for the twenty-first century. They successfully engaged school districts, educational organizations, families, communities, higher education, business and labor, and the governor and state legislature in developing a ten-year vision to meet the state's four learning goals for each student:

▪ Read with comprehension, write with skill, and communicate effectively and responsibly in a variety of ways and settings.
▪ Know and apply the core concepts and principles of mathematics; social, physical, and life sciences; civics and history; geography; arts; and health and fitness.
▪ Think analytically, logically, and creatively and integrate experiences and knowledge to form reasoned judgments and solve problems.
▪ Understand the importance of work and how performance, effort, and decisions directly affect career and educational opportunities.

This vision is rapidly becoming a reality. Recently, the state legislature approved three extra staff-development days to develop performance standards. Also because hiring and retaining good teachers is essential, pay increases for existing teachers and a 15 percent pay increase for new teachers were approved. Finally, improvements were also legislated for new technology, teacher certification, and a safe-schools program in which students are taught mediation and have access to support networks—including an adult advocate for every child.

Jonelle Adams, the executive director for the Washington Alliance for Better Schools, said that what made the large group sessions and walkthrus successful was the attention they paid to working by democratic principles. In simple yet profound ways, they incorporated these principles into the design of each session. The very first large group session started with a discussion of purpose, and then asked participants to consider what it would be like if they were to incorporate the principles of egalitarian spirit, co-creation of the future, and public information and decision making in their work together. The power of these principles grabbed people and rapidly became the guiding light for everything that followed.

The 150 stakeholders represented research and information, curriculum instruction, pre-service, technology, staff development, and high-performance organizations. They developed plans and processes, shared them with each other, received feedback, and then refined and adjusted their proposals over the course of two 2-day large group sessions. Recognizing that they would not be successful unless they widened the circle of involvement, each stakeholder group took responsibility for sharing the results of the session and obtaining feedback from their peers across the state. The information they gathered was used to refine their plans. This process produced not only a better set of initiatives, but a critical mass of people who were behind their work. When it came time to meet with the state legislature, they knew they were not alone. As Jonelle recounts, "If we did not have the support and backing we achieved through this process, we would not have stood a chance with the legislature."

Summary

Embracing democracy really is the hard part of the process. However, its difficulty should not deter you from applying this principle—it is critical to the success of the engagement paradigm. Embracing democracy is a principle in its own right and a thread that runs through all the other principles. It requires leaders to open up the information-sharing and decision-making processes and listen for understanding, while at the same time supporting equity and fairness and increasing freedom and autonomy throughout the organization. Leaders who are under extreme pressure to produce results and control the outcomes may experience this as a daunting task. However, it is a task that cannot be ignored.

PART 3

Getting Started

7

When Engagement Disengages
Some Words of Caution Before You Begin

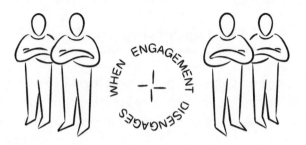

This is the "buyer beware" chapter. There is a downside to engagement: when it goes wrong, cynicism and doubt become epidemic. Engagement is powerful and seductive because it taps into people's desire to shape their own destiny, to be part of something larger than themselves, to make a difference. For organizations that are characterized by top-down or paternalistic leadership styles, engagement carries with it the fresh air of power and freedom. Having overcome their initial distrust of engaging in the change process and having breathed the fresh air of engagement, people will not go back willingly. Moreover, when leaders renege on the promise of engagement, the damage that occurs often takes years to repair. Organizations that create false, manipulative engagement strategies or cancel their engagement processes in midstream are actually worse off than those that never start.

Additionally, despite my enthusiasm for the engagement paradigm, I know that it has a shadow side. (A psychological concept originally developed by noted psychiatrist Carl Jung, the *shadow* is defined as the negative aspects of ourselves that we would just as soon not consider—the parts of ourselves that we do not own as we attempt to project a positive image of ourselves to the world.) In the work context, these parts can be the desire to control others, manipulate outcomes, or to win at any cost. The shadow side of the engagement paradigm has three components: one is the behavior of leaders as they move away from top-down or paternalistic styles, one involves the engagement strategies, and the third relates to the paradigm itself.

The Leadership Shadow

Current change management practices have created a healthy degree of cynicism regarding organizational change processes. Many people, with good reason, experience these processes as manipulative attempts to get them to do something against their will. Their feelings of betrayal and insult are voiced when they say, "Why don't they just tell us what they want us to do? Don't ask me for my opinion when there is only one right answer—the boss's. If my voice doesn't count, please don't waste my time."

Leaders who embrace the engagement paradigm are often surprised when their initial efforts to engage the organization are met with such distrust. What they fail to recognize is the impact of their previous behavior on the organization. When people express dissatisfaction, they are holding up a mirror that reflects a true image of their organizational experience. Leaders often perceive this reflection as flawed, presenting a distorted view of reality like one of those carnival mirrors that make tall, thin people look short and fat. They do not realize that, in reality, this mirror is reflecting back to them their shadow side.

Leaders who use the engagement paradigm often wish to see themselves and be seen by the organization as enlightened executives who have the best interests of the organization and its stakeholders at heart. They see themselves as increasing organizational performance using leading-edge methodologies that bring out the best in people. Having made the decision to use the engagement paradigm, they often suffer from the delusion that they have already made the necessary changes in leadership style and behavior to operate effectively in this paradigm. Rather than seeing themselves as part of the change process and as needing to change themselves, they think they have already made the transition and it is others who need to change. This is rarely the case.

Since most leaders have not previously employed the engagement paradigm, they are novices at using it. Unfortunately, they often become trapped in the organization's expectation that they of course know how to use the engagement paradigm by virtue of the fact that they are leaders. Having bought into this assumption, leaders take shortcuts in the change process. If the process calls for education and training, leaders always get the executive summary or "short course"— when they may require as much education and training as others, or more. Three-day training sessions become reduced to half-day briefings, and leaders are told they need to attend only parts of conferences, workshops, or meetings because they are smart, busy people. Additionally, their power in the organization makes lower-level members timid in their presence and so people hesitate to make the demands necessary for success. Instead, they make requests that leaders might readily accept. This collusion between leader arrogance (because I am the leader, I already know how to engage the organization) and staff timidity is a recipe for disaster.

This is just one facet of the leadership shadow. There are other components:

- Violations of trust
- Violations of equity and fairness
- Conversations that disengage
- Discounting behaviors
- Ignoring past organizational damage
- Loss of will or willingness to implement

Violations of Trust

Trust is a precious commodity. We can think of it as money in the "relationship bank." As we work with people over time, deposits are made. We learn when someone gives us their word that we can count on it or that when they make commitments, these commitments are kept. We learn through working with them that we can count on them for straight talk and reliable action. When we have worked with someone over time and they have built up a trust account with us, if they are suddenly less than candid or they do not meet a commitment, we are likely to give them the benefit of the doubt. However, there is a point at which the balance in the relationship bank becomes depleted and trust changes to mistrust. That is the point at which people begin to disengage from the relationship. For leaders with little or no money in the relationship bank, disengagement occurs sooner than for those who have a rich relationship account.

John Carter, who is on the faculty of the Gestalt Institute in Cleveland, Ohio, has developed a model for thinking about trust that is useful for those leaders who do not wish to run the risk of violating the trust of their organization (see Figure 7-1.) He calls it the *trust triangle.*

The foundation of the triangle is straight talk. Straight talk means sharing all the information available in an honest and forthright manner. It does not mean doling out partial truths or sharing only the in-

Figure 7-1 The Trust Triangle

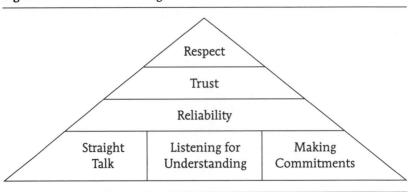

formation that supports a point of view or course of action. It means providing all the available facts, your thoughts and feelings about those facts, and what you would like to have happen. When leaders hold back on any component of straight talk, they risk breaching trust.

Straight talk must be accompanied by listening for understanding. When we listen for understanding, we not only gain more information, others trust us more. For more on this idea, see "Attentive Listening" later in this chapter, in the section titled "Conversations That Disengage."

The next component of the triangle is making commitments. When we make a commitment, we are pledging ourselves to a course of action. Trust is built when commitments are kept. Sometimes commitments are made that cannot be kept. Because leaders are often embarrassed about this, they fail to say or do anything about it, hoping that it will just go away instead of dealing with the issue directly. When commitments just disappear, trust is broken. What is necessary to avoid this outcome is for leaders to use straight talk to explain what happened and why their commitment, made in good faith, cannot be kept.

The next component of trust is to become reliable over time. This means doing what you say you are going to do. It means that you are true to your word and that people can count on you. This is an extension of making commitments. When organization members can put faith in their leaders to both make and keep commitments, these leaders become reliable over time.

When leaders engage in straight talk, listen for understanding, make commitments, and become reliable over time, they become trustworthy and are able to engage the organization in change.

There is an equally straightforward list of actions that make leaders untrustworthy:

- They speak half-truths, do not provide complete information, or do not share their true intentions.
- They make commitments they do not intend to keep or commitments they do not understand.
- They cannot be relied upon to keep the promises they make.

When leaders violate trust, they produce disengagement.

Violations of Equity and Fairness

When leaders violate principles of equity and fairness they are saying that there is one set of rules for the elite and another set of rules for those who are participating in the change process. This mind-set creates hierarchical divisions and cliques, breaks connections between people, prevents communities from acting, and violates democratic principles. It pushes people away from the change process.

Unwillingness to engage personally in the change process is a classic violation of equity and fairness. This is a direct result of the belief discussed at the beginning of the chapter that leaders already have their act together and it is up to the organization to make the necessary changes. When leaders take this aristocratic approach to change, they are leading in a way that is incongruent with the principles of the engagement paradigm. It is no wonder that their behavior is often met with cynicism and scorn.

A classic example of unwillingness to participate is the leader who kicks off a meeting or workshop, then goes on to do other things only to return at the end of the session to bless the outcomes. This lack of engagement in the process engenders skepticism and mistrust about the leader's true intentions and the importance of the group's own efforts. Leaders who do not engage in the co-creation process never become part of the community.

A variation of this behavior is exhibited by leaders who show up midsession between other meetings they regard as too important to miss. Feeling that their time is limited, they hurry to influence the change process. They operate from a fear that unless the organization has their input, people will make serious errors in judgment. And not knowing what preceded their lightning visit or what is to follow, they act like the proverbial bull in the china shop, making comments out of context and damaging the process.

In both instances, the leaders are saying that engagement is for you, not for me. I am too busy, too important, to spend time with you on this project that I have said is crucial to the organization's success. These violations of egalitarian spirit cause people to disengage from the change process.

Another way leaders violate equity and fairness is by attempting to reengineer operating portions of the organization while the top remains unchanged. In addition to its technical problems, this produces a separation between the organization and its leaders. It is impossible for organization leaders to understand and have empathy for those going through the change process unless they are personally involved and submit themselves to the same vulnerabilities and risks they are asking other members of the organization to take. It is one thing to ask people to change, knowing that your job and role are secure, and it is another thing to participate equally with people in the change process. How many reengineering projects have asked organization members to participate in the redesign of processes and structures while exempting senior leadership from the process? How many leaders have clung to the secure knowledge that their own position is excluded from the process while asking organization members to potentially reengineer themselves out of jobs? What if leaders and organization members shared the same vulnerability during organizational change processes? Not participating equally produces disengagement; participating and sharing the same risks with others produces engagement.

Other examples of violations of equity and fairness include

- Selection procedures that prevent certain groups of people from participating in the change process.
- Decisions that are made behind closed doors.
- Decision-making processes that are unclear.

Conversations That Disengage

The failure to listen is another behavior that disengages rather than engages. In *The Intelligence Advantage: Organizing for Complexity,* Michael D. McMaster states: "The ability to listen in its broadest sense, is at the heart of engagement. . . . Engagement is expressing oneself- and listening to the expression of others. . . . Engagement is thinking, inquiring, and exploring possibility." Because of its significance in the engagement process, it is worthwhile to explore the aspects of listening and speaking that produce engagement in depth.

Attentive Listening

Listening for understanding builds relationships, while listening to get your own way creates distance. Typically, when leaders hear organization members expressing dissatisfaction with the change process, they immediately label them as complainers or resisters who must be won over. The leader usually listens only long enough to formulate a counterargument and then proceeds to defend the original position, thereby cutting off potentially valuable information and discounting the other person's opinion. There is an alternative that engages people in the change process. It is called *attentive listening.* Attentive listening was developed by Sherrod and Phyllis Miller, authors of *Core Communication: Skills and Processes,* and is based on the concepts of creating understanding and building relationships.

Attentive listening means creating a relationship with those you are listening to in which they experience being completely heard and understood. You may believe that you are a good listener and that you readily understand what others are saying. However, your assessment is not the one that counts. It is how others experience you that matters. When leaders listen only long enough to formulate counterarguments, people experience themselves as being in a debate rather than in an understanding environment. When someone expresses doubt, if you listen so that you can convince them that their doubts are unfounded, then you are not listening with the intention of understanding. When you listen with the intention of convincing, you lose an opportunity to gain essential information.

A critical concept in attentive listening is *understanding first and agreement second.* First understand the other person's point of view. That is the main concern and it is where we need to focus our attention. Then, once there is an understanding of the viewpoints, we can enter a discussion regarding agreements or disagreements. There is always time to find agreement or to deal with disagreement. However, when we try to reach agreement without first understanding each other, we miss a crucial opportunity for gathering information that can lead to engagement. Once two parties get into a debate, each trying to win the other over, the ability to learn information that could actually improve the change process rapidly diminishes.

Attentive listening means understanding the issue as if you were standing in the other person's shoes. It means looking at the world through their eyes. How do they see the situation? What are their experiences? What are their hopes and fears?

Attentive listening is a complex series of integrated skills. Here are some pointers for becoming an attentive listener:

▪ *Start with intentionality.* What are your intentions? What do you want to be different for you, for the other person, and for the relationship? If you could imagine this conversation going exactly the way you would like, what would happen? Would you understand the other person's point of view, or would you have convinced them to agree with you? These are radically different intentions that have radically different outcomes. Listening for understanding creates trust and safety. Listening so that you can convince someone to come to your side produces defensiveness. The worst possible situation occurs when you publicly state your intention to understand others and you behave in a way that is experienced as trying to win them over to your side. This mixed message creates apprehension and a distrustful environment.

▪ *Listen for the history.* What has happened in the past that has caused these people to think or feel the way they do? Recently my colleagues and I were with people who had worked on a sugar plantation in Hawaii. They spoke fondly of the days when they were plantation workers. What they remembered was the sense of community among the workers and their families: how they would help each other and be supportive of each other. We would never have predicted that people would speak fondly of working on a plantation, but there it was. The group's strong sense of community was born in the days on the plantation and their yearning for a sense of community today had its roots in that past.

▪ *Listen for thoughts.* What interpretations have the other people made about their history? Everyone's experience colors how they see the same set of facts. One has only to look at recent controversies surrounding our political leaders to recognize how people can look at the same set of facts and come to widely different conclusions.

■ *Listen for facts.* What data do the other people have that causes them to think and feel the way they do? Facts are the raw, observable data. They are different from thoughts. The facts are what actually happened, which is different from what we think happened or how we feel about what happened. Remember the old radio and TV drama *Dragnet?* Sergeant Friday was concerned only with the facts.

■ *Listen for feelings.* What emotions do the others have? Are they feeling sad, happy, glad, or excited? Listening for feelings means being able to understand and even to some extent experience the feelings of others. When a person experiences being understood at the feeling level, a new connection is made with the listener and trust is increased. This is a tremendously powerful experience.

■ *Listen for intentions again.* Now listen for the other people's intentions again and you will come to understand what they want to have happen for themselves, for you, and for the relationship. When you come to understand their intentions, you will understand why they are saying what they are saying and doing what they are doing. There will be coherence between your interpretation of other people's intentions and their actual intentions. Often our story about others' intentions—for example, they are trying to sabotage the change effort—is only a story. Their intention may actually be to have the process succeed. They just do not want to do it in the way you are proposing.

What does attentive listening look like when it works?

You have just presented your case for change to a group of employees and you are fielding questions from the floor. A hand goes up and a belligerent voice says, "I think you guys are just manipulating us!" Your first impulse is to kick the guy out of the room and your second is to convince him of the rightness of your cause. You take a deep breath and say to yourself, "What do I really want to have happen here?" And a voice from within says, "I want to understand why he feels the way he does." So you respond by saying, "You seem upset. Could you tell me why you feel that way?" He answers, "Damn right I'm upset. This the fifth reorganization we have had in the last five years and nothing gets any better. All that happens is that we move people around and all we get from management is broken promises." And you respond by saying, "I think if I were in your shoes, I would feel the same way. In fact, I'm not satisfied with what we've done in the past." He replies, in a calmer voice, "We have plenty of problems around here but no one ever asks us what to do about them. I would like to see things improved and I have some ideas." You encourage him: "We need your ideas and I hope that you will join us and help us turn this organization around." And he says in a quiet voice, "Well, maybe I'll try it this time."

Through attentive listening, the speaker came to understand the fear and anger that our belligerent friend in the audience was expressing. The leader avoided the temptation to punish the speaker or to try to convince him that the new plan would work when others had failed. His only intention was to listen and understand the speaker's point of view. He therefore turned a potentially explosive situation into a positive opportunity. In doing so, he was able to create a situation in which a person who was disengaged from the change process took one small step toward engagement.

Strategies and Structures for Listening

Leaders who use the attentive listening skills outlined in the preceding section gain new intelligence about what is happening in the organization. However, more is required than just individual effort. For a change process to succeed, there must be structures and strategies for allowing fears to surface and be understood.

A typical change effort starts out with management holding meetings about the change and making the case for change. People are lined up theater-style to get the word. These briefings usually last an hour, with the leaders speaking for about fifty minutes and then asking if there are any questions. Typically, the silence is deafening. The leaders and attendees leave the meeting frustrated. The leaders feel that they have not been able to get their message across and the attendees leave with unanswered questions and unexpressed doubts and fears.

Here is an alternative scenario. The leaders give a brief overview of the change process, why they are doing it, why they are doing it now, and why they are using a highly participative change strategy. People are sitting at round tables and have briefing materials in front of them. After the overview, the leaders finish their presentation with these questions: What did you hear us saying? What are your questions and concerns? Each table then meets for fifteen minutes and discusses the questions. The tables are then called on and a dialogue occurs between the leadership and those in attendance. The leaders use attentive listening skills and present honest information. When they do not know the answer, they say so. At the end of the hour, the room is buzzing with conversation. Everyone leaves with a mixture of excitement about the potential and concerned about what needs to happen in order to make the change a reality.

Meetings like this must be held periodically during the change process, not just at the beginning. The walkthru process described in Chapter Two is a both a structure and a strategy for increasing communication and understanding the fears that are part and parcel of every change process.

A Guarantee

If you practice attentive listening and create structures and strategies where attentive listening can occur, not only will you gain a new understanding of the concerns of those you have been labeling as resistant, you will create the conditions for engagement. Additionally, you will gain information that will inform you about how your strategy may need to change in order to be successful. Listening deeply, without the intention to change another person's point of view, will allow discussions to occur that will produce new possibilities. You might argue that this level of listening takes more time than you have to spend. My response is, you can spend the time in listening and creating engagement, or you can spend the time in dealing with a disengaged organization. The choice is yours.

Conversations That Engage

A companion to attentive listening is straight talk. Together, these are the foundations for creating conversations that engage. As noted earlier, straight talk is an essential component of trust. It is the clear expression of your thoughts, feelings, intentions, and wants. However, this is not a one-way conversation. Straight talk means sharing information in a way that allows for the expression of the other person's thoughts, feelings, intentions, and wants as well. It is based on respect for the other person's point of view. It is through this mutual expression and information sharing that new possibilities occur. Straight talk and attentive listening create possibilities, while conversations that exclude these critical dimensions close down possibilities.

Engagement is an open conversation of possibilities. Disengagement is a one-way conversation of selling and coercion.

Discounting Behaviors

Discounting behaviors are behaviors that say *I count and you do not.* Some are obvious and others are subtle, but the result is the same—they push people away rather than drawing them in. Here are some examples.

One subtle form of discounting is bringing other work in to a meeting. When leaders read their mail or bring other work to meetings, they are saying that these memos and letters are far more important than what is going on in the meeting. Whoever does this may see it as a form of multi-tasking, but in fact it discounts the work of the other people in the room.

Another way to discount others is to talk over them, interrupt, and quash their input. The message here is that what I have to say is far more important than anything you may have to say.

Spending time out in the hall talking to others or on the phone when a meeting is going on is disrespectful of those who are present and ready to work. This behavior shows a disregard for the group, communicating the message that what I am doing right now is more important than the task of the group. A corollary to this behavior is habitual tardiness. This shows a disrespect for the time and efforts of those who were ready to go at the appointed time.

Obvious examples of discounting are the trappings of organizational power that let people know how important an executive's position is. They include but are not limited to private parking places and garages and private meeting spaces.

Conferences and meetings during which the majority of time is devoted to leaders and experts talking to the audience are further examples of discounting. Even if these sessions include time for questions and answers, the roles are clear: questions can come only from those in the audience and answers can come only from those on the podium. It goes even further: Those on the podium are usually the only ones equipped with microphones. Why should those on the podium have microphones? Are they the only ones whose voices are worth amplifying?

Conference rooms with long rectangular tables are powerful statements of who counts and who does not. Those at the head of the table have the best sight lines and can take in the whole group, while those along the side have limited views. The seating arrangement dictated by these tables lets everyone know who counts and who doesn't. Even when leaders take seats on the sides of the tables, the impact of this seating arrangement remains. What if you replaced all the rectangular conference tables in your organization with round tables? Tables whose very shape speaks to egalitarianism and everyone having an equal voice. You might argue, just changing the table is not enough. I agree with you, but by changing the table, you make a powerful statement about the kind of interactions and relationships you want to occur within your organization. Try it and see what a difference it makes.

These are just a few examples of discounting behaviors that disengage. I am sure that you can add to this list by taking a few minutes to think about times when you feel that you don't count and identifying the behaviors that contribute to these feelings.

Ignoring Past Organizational Damage

In today's world, there is hardly an organization that has not tried to introduce change by using some form of employee participation. Typically, these efforts start out with great fanfare only to fade away months later when they are replaced with the latest change initiative. With each of these change processes, hope grows anew: This change process will really make a difference, this time someone will really involve us in a meaningful way. And time after time these hopes are dashed on the rocks of expediency as the old change process makes way for the new, leaving behind employees who grow more hardened and resentful by the day.

Damage can be caused in other ways. It can come from leaders who fail to share information, or share information that is not false but not completely truthful, or who are outright deceitful. It can come from leadership decisions that make people wonder if anyone really knows what is going on.

No matter what the cause, this kind of damage is a reality in many organizations today. When leaders ignore this truth, they sow the seeds of disengagement. The seduction of any new change process, the engagement paradigm included, is what leads many organizations and their leaders to overlook the damage that has already been done. Often they know the damage exists but the new change process promises to take care of the mistakes of the past. For example, an earlier change process may not have included enough people and so leaders believe the engagement paradigm is the remedy. However, in embracing the engagement paradigm as something that will overcome the problems with previous change initiatives, you may be discounting the lingering effects of these problems on your organization.

Dealing with organizational damage is essential to the success of the engagement paradigm. As part of the change process, it is crucial that leaders examine their history with previous change processes in order to determine what worked and what did not. Have past attempts left organization members feeling resentful over dashed hopes and broken promises, or are they optimistic about the possibilities because of past successes? While the engagement paradigm can help repair organizational damage, it is essential that leaders spend time assessing the current level of damage, then develop strategies with organization members that identify what needs to be done differently in this change process.

Consider for a moment this common example: In a manufacturing organization, employees feel that the input they provided during the previous change process has been ignored. Change processes have been implemented that disregard their ideas and suggestions without explanation. It is essential that leaders understand why the employees feel this way and what it was about the change process that contributed to this damage. Then collectively with organization members, they should develop processes and procedures that provide for sharing the outcomes of the change process. It is critical that organization members be able to track their input all the way through the process to the point of implementation. It is essential that they understand the reasons why plans were adopted or rejected.

It is impossible to overemphasize the extent to which violations of trust, lack of equity and fairness, and a leader's inability to listen disengage people and damage an organization. Likewise, it is astonishing how effective it is to genuinely reverse these behaviors. Here is a real-life example:

A hospital was about to adopt the engagement paradigm to improve patient care. Before the start of the process, focus groups were conducted. The purpose of these interviews was to identify those forces within the organization that supported the change process and those forces within the organization that could prevent the change process from being successful. One of the important findings was that employees did not trust senior leaders. They believed that they did not get timely, complete information, and that senior leadership did not tell the truth. Furthermore, they were skeptical about senior leaders' commitment to implement the changes they would recommend. They felt that previous attempts to involve them in change had been fruitless and did not see what was different about this process. Employees experienced their good ideas as disappearing into a Bermuda Triangle, never to hear about them again.

Recognizing that these feelings would lead to disengagement rather than engagement, the senior leadership of the organization developed a strategy to increase trust. The strategy was simple enough. It consisted of being brutally honest. Straight talk was the watchword. The leaders were also fanatic about keeping the commitments they made. And in those few instances when commitments needed revision or changing, they communicated effectively with the organization about what changed and the reasons why they were unable to keep their commitments. They then developed new action plans with those affected by the change. Throughout the process, they emphasized listening rather than telling and used meetings similar to the one described in the listening section to help repair the damage that was present in the organization. Over a two-year period, they have worked diligently to apply these behaviors and adhere to the principles of the engagement paradigm. This has resulted in organizational changes that have increased patient satisfaction, improved clinical quality, and reduced costs.

Loss of Will or Willingness to Implement

Consider the following scenario: The company has employed the engagement paradigm and followed the ideas and precepts contained in this book. Its managers have engaged large numbers of their employees, customers, and suppliers in creating a new way of doing business. In fact, business is so good it is a problem. The company is growing so fast that the biggest problem now facing the organization is making sure that there are enough desks and telephones for everyone.

Meanwhile, there is a dark cloud on the horizon. Members of the leadership team are struggling to keep their heads above water as market demands for the services this organization provides increase exponentially. Soon they begin to resent the work the engagement paradigm requires. Meeting attendance is sparse. Planning meetings are postponed because of other pressing issues and are rarely rescheduled. Leaders who are members of the planning committee now begin to complain aloud about the time and effort the change process requires. Slowly, the process grinds to a halt. The leaders have abandoned the change process that had successfully engaged their organization, leaving in its wake disappointment, disillusionment, and disengagement. They no longer have the will or the willingness to implement the process.

When leaders use the engagement paradigm, it is critical that they think through the implications of their choice. Because the engagement paradigm widens the circle of involvement, they have huge visibility. When a few people are working on a change initiative that is halted, these few may be devastated, but the organization can continue to function. This is nothing like what happens when you have involved hundreds or thousands of people in a change process only to have it disappear off the radar screen. It is essential that leaders understand the magnitude of what they are undertaking and ask themselves if they have both the will and the willingness to implement the results. It is far better not to start than to stop in midstream and consequently disengage those very people you sought to engage in the first place. In the company cursed by success, the leaders did not start out intending to stop in midstream, but when they did, enormous organizational damage ensued. Had they taken a few minutes of self-examination to understand the magnitude of the change they were undertaking and whether they had the time and energy to follow through, a different result might have occurred.

The Strategy Shadow

Engagement strategies that disengage are different from leadership behaviors in that the disengagement occurs as a result of the strategy itself rather than the individual behavior. These design flaws produce withdrawal and cynicism. Here are examples of how engagement strategies can disengage:

- Process designed to manipulate rather than engage
- Unclear decision-making rules
- Unclear boundaries between what's in and what's out
- Selective information sharing
- Violations of equity and fairness

Processes Designed to Manipulate Rather Than Engage

My colleagues and I are often approached by prospective clients with requests like this: "We want to do something that makes people feel as if they have a voice in the future." The language of the statement represents the depth of the issue. *Feeling as if you have a voice is altogether different from actually having a voice.* This may seem like a trivial semantic difference, but it is not. Our experience is that when potential clients come to us with this type of request, they are usually saying something like: "We already know what we want to do. We have the answers. We want to develop a process whereby employees feel as if they were involved and created the outcome. We want people to come up with an answer that we have already determined and we do not want to let people know what that answer is ahead of time." This is out-and-out manipulation. Trying to use the engagement paradigm and other related processes to make people think they have choice and involvement when in fact they do not sows the seeds of disengagement.

Again, McMaster provides valuable insights about how manipulation disengages:

> Engagement does not emerge from intentions of manipulation and selling. The difference between selling and engagement is like the difference between conscription and voluntary labor, manipulation and invitation, or dictatorship and leadership. Selling and manipulation, in the context of management, are dehumanizing ways of interacting with people; whereas engagement represents a respectful and humanizing relationship to those around us. . . . When we are manipulating people, it implies that they have nothing to say about what is occurring and most human beings tend to resist that idea. It implies that people are being related to as tools of some kind.

In short, manipulation disengages.

Unclear Decision-Making Rules

Essential to the success of the engagement paradigm is a clear understanding of the rules by which decisions are made and adopted. Although my bias is to make decisions using the democratic processes described in Chapter Six, what is even more important is for the decision-making ground rules to be clear and explicit. What I hear over and over again from organization members is their sense of outrage when they believed that they were participating in a process where they had an equal voice in the decision making only to find out later that there was only one vote that counted. The boss's vote. In these cases, those employing an engagement strategy are playing a high-stakes game. They are taking the chance that those involved will come up with an answer that is acceptable to the leader. If they are lucky, the group does and this strategy works. Everyone feels good for the wrong reasons. The leader feels good because it wasn't necessary to invoke authority to get the group to go along with the pre-selected solution. The group members feel good because they think they have had real influence in shaping the future. When those in the decision-making process do not come up with the leader's solution, then the leader must stop the process and tell those involved what's really going to happen. Predictably, feelings of anger and betrayal from those involved emerge and disengagement follows.

Unclear Boundaries

With a false sense of openness, those developing engagement strategies are reluctant to put limits on the process. When asked whether they want to impose limits or boundaries, their immediate response is that there are none. Fearing to limit creativity, or overreacting to feelings in the organization that there is already a preconceived solution, they embark on the change process without mapping the terrain. In doing so, they foster further disengagement.

Change processes without boundaries become too big, making it difficult for people to get their arms around the issues. Since few of us live in a world without limits, the idea of unlimited change is not credible. On the other hand, when the limits or boundaries are narrowly drawn, those involved throw up their hands, saying, "Why bother? They already know what they want. I do not want to waste my time on this." Disengagement occurs when boundaries are either too big or too small.

The trick in setting boundaries is to make them big enough so that they provide enough room for people to make a difference and give the change process a shape or direction. Providing clear boundaries lets participants know the limits of the process they are participating in and the rules of the game.

Here is an example of a set of goals and boundaries used by a manufacturing organization that successfully used the engagement paradigm for organizational redesign:

Goals

- Seven percent improvement in process reliability
- Reduction of controllable cost by $15 per unit of output
- Customer satisfaction improvements to the 98 percent level on the customer-satisfaction survey
- Create a world class safety environment

Boundaries

- The new organization must be capable of meeting the above-mentioned goals.
- The new organization must assure a safe and healthful work environment.
- Work designs will advance business needs and strategies as they apply to customers, product quality and mix, and profitability, and they will be mutually beneficial to employees.
- Any personnel reductions entailed will be consistent with the labor agreement as amended.
- Work-design changes will be consistent with the labor agreement as amended. Should the work-design propose changes to the labor agreement or company policy, these changes will be referred to the enabling team, negotiating team, or company officials as appropriate.

Here is a set of boundaries developed by a hospital for its engagement process:

Goals

- Reduce cost: Reduce patient care delivery costs by $2 million annually by November 1997, through improved efficiency and productivity.

- Improve quality: Enhance clinical outcomes by integrating processes and better coordinating care.
- Improve satisfaction: Improve satisfaction among our patients, volunteers, physicians, and employees.
- Promote culture change: Build a framework to enable responsiveness to the changing health care world based in high employee participation.

Boundaries

- Be consistent with the organization's strategic plan.
- Meet regulatory, accreditation, and legal requirements.
- Focus on the process of "Service and Care Delivery."
- Follow the normal approval processes for operational and capital expenses.
- Negotiate job-related issues through normal channels.
- Have policies and practices in place to support individuals who may be displaced as a result of redesign, utilizing principles of attrition, retraining to facility positions where practical, reemployment assistance, and adequate notification.

Here are the goals and guidelines used by a chemical company to create a new product development process.

Goals

- Customer satisfaction: Anticipate customer needs and furnish solutions that promote customer success.
- Market leadership: Create products and services that redefine industries, that change the basis of competition in the markets we serve.
- Speed and success rate: Dramatically increase the speed of creation and commercialization of products and services.
- Profitability: Improve our operating profit level to the level of the industry leaders.
- Employee fulfillment: Ensure that all team members have ownership of the process from start to finish. Instill pride and camaraderie as shown by teamwork and positive work relationships.

■ Knowledge utilization: Use technology to leverage our impact. Learn and use our customers' knowledge of their markets and technology.

Boundaries

■ Warranty: The goals are to bring better and more creative solutions to the customers at a faster rate, be an industry leader, and enable us to grow our business profitably. Job reduction is not a goal and is not anticipated.

■ Scope of the product development process: From anticipation or identification of customers' needs to commercialization.

■ Product enhancements: From minor adjustments to product replacements.

■ Organization structure: The current team structure will be maintained. The use and deployment of product-development resources within the company is open for discussion.

■ Business strategy: The overall business strategy is not included in this process, but all business and product lines are open for discussion with regard to the product-development process.

Principles of Operation

■ Incorporate the organization's vision and values.
■ Customer satisfaction is our ultimate goal.
■ Quality products and services.
■ A learning organization.
■ Diverse people and perspectives.
■ Open and honest communications.
■ Responsible care.
■ Meet established capital and economic requirements.
■ Process changes must be capable of being implemented this year.

Selective Information Sharing

Strategies that provide for limited information sharing create distrust. The heightened anxiety that accompanies most change processes creates an increased demand for information. But at the very time when more information is needed, organizations choose to limit information out of a fear of contributing incomplete information to an already overflowing rumor mill. Unfortunately for these companies, the information in the rumor mill is far more damaging and disengaging than anything that could possibly be shared by the organization.

A cornerstone of the engagement paradigm is the free flow of information among everyone in the organization. To that end, the *data-assist team* (a group of employees who summarize data from large group sessions, conduct walkthrus, and gather feedback for incorporation in the change process) plays a critical role in providing an information conduit to the organization, providing a bridge between the large group sessions and those who were unable to attend these sessions. In addition to the data-assist team, formal and informal discussions with leaders; multimedia, multi-channel, and intranet presentations; and even Internet sites aimed at outside stakeholders are critical to the success of any change process.

Violations of Equity and Fairness

Leaders aren't alone in the ability to violate equity and fairness principles by their behavior. It is also possible for the very design of the change process to contain fundamental flaws when it comes to equity and fairness. Four essential questions relate to these principles: Who gets to participate? How are participants chosen? How are decisions made? Who will be affected by the change process?

A classic violation of these principles occurs when deciding who will participate in the change process. When the decision about who gets to participate is closed, and when it results in the same people creating the new direction for the rest of the organization, organization members disengage and the seeds of resistance are sown. Having been blocked from the opportunity to participate in the new direction, organization members may even engage in acts of sabotage.

Throughout this book, I have advocated change processes that provide equal opportunity for everyone to participate, including those who are opposed and are resistant. The decision about who gets to participate is fair and equitable when it uses the selection criteria described in Chapter Three. It is only when the whole system is represented in the change process that strategies can be developed that represent all points of view.

Connected to the decision of who gets to participate is the question of how people are selected to participate. Hand-selecting all the participants engages those who are selected and disengages those not selected. It is crucial that the process for selecting participants to the change process be seen as fair and equitable. Knowing that you had an equal chance to participate is as important as actually ending up as one of the participants.

Including those who are affected by the change is essential to success. Not only does this improve the decision quality because those closest to the work are designing changes to the work, it increases ownership and commitment. The mind-set shifts from apprehension to excitement as people move from being outsiders to being part and parcel of the change process.

The natural fallback during times of stress and tension is to overdesign the change process so that the desired outcomes are guaranteed. Typically, this occurs when the boundaries that are created are so tight that they can lead to only one outcome. When this happens people disengage because they feel manipulated by the process. They are told that their ideas are needed and anything is possible, but on closer inspection of the process, they see that the boundaries dictate only one possible solution. Feeling manipulated, they disengage. If there can be only one course of action and that course of action has already been determined, it is far better to state that publicly than pretend that people have a choice.

The Engagement Paradigm's Own Shadow

Every change process has its positive and negative attributes. I have devoted a lot of space to the negative aspects of the top-down and change management paradigms, and my enthusiasm may well have made it appear that I see no negative aspects in the engagement paradigm—but perfection is no more true of the engagement paradigm than of any other human system. It does have negative aspects, which represent potential blind spots that must be made visible in order for it to be successful. Table 7-1 represents a comparison of the positive and negative aspects of the three paradigms.

There are four negative attributes to the engagement paradigm. The first is that it is more chaotic than other paradigms. This is a result of involving more people and having more open decision-making processes. Other change processes try to guard against these feelings of chaos by limiting the involvement and decision-making authority of those involved. The engagement paradigm embraces the chaos and confusion that occurs when more people and points of view are included. Successful implementation requires leaders who can live with the ambiguity that is part and parcel of the engagement paradigm.

The second negative aspect is that it requires leaders to profoundly let go of prerogatives. This means letting go of decisions that are made by leaders and leaders alone, such as the specific outcomes of the change process, who will be involved in creating those changes, and in many cases the final say about whether or not to adopt a proposed course of action. Every leader that I have known has said that the leader's ability to let go is the critical success factor when using the engagement paradigm. But they are not talking about abdication, they are talking about letting go enough to deeply engage the organization in setting new directions. Indeed, some have described their experience using the engagement paradigm as a course in learning how to let go without abdicating.

A third negative aspect is that the engagement paradigm requires a higher level of initial investment. As change processes move from the few to the many, the initial costs increase. It is not unusual for the cost of large group sessions that engage large numbers of employees to be substantial. These costs are more visible than the hidden costs of dealing with the resistance that is generated by the other paradigms. Thus they often create pressure for quick results because of the huge up-front investment. This pressure for results often causes

Table 7-1 Comparison of Three Change Paradigms

	Top-Down Paradigm	Change-Management Paradigm	Engagement Paradigm
Positive Aspects	• Clear direction • Leaders stay in charge • Decisions can be made quickly • Everyone knows what leadership wants	• Diverse participation • Reduction in bureaucracy • System orientation • Builds ownership and commitment	• High involvement speeds implementation • Whole-system involvement produces high-quality, integrated solutions • Democratic principles build trust, create commitment, and increase creativity • Increases organizational capacity to change
Negative Aspects	• Creates resistance from those not involved • Decisions lack critical information from those at lower levels	• Emphasis on only the best and brightest participating • Often increases bureaucracy rather than reducing it • Involves relatively few people, thereby creating "in groups" and "out groups"	• Is more chaotic than other paradigms • Requires leaders to let go of prerogatives • Requires a higher initial investment of people and resources • Is more visible than other paradigms

leaders to take shortcuts or to try to compromise the principles of the paradigm.

The fourth aspect is similar to the third. When you engage more people in the change process, it becomes more visible. It is hard to ignore a change process that involves large numbers of people. When the change process moves out from behind closed doors into the light of day, it attracts attention. This increased attention puts pressure on leaders and those designing the change process. They come under a high level of scrutiny. Again, this pressure sometimes causes people to abandon the principles of the paradigm in an effort to protect themselves against criticism and create outcomes that are more predictable. This behavior is just the opposite of what is needed. What is required is for those leading the change processes to make sure that their behavior and the design of the change process stays congruent with the principles of the engagement paradigm. When leaders design processes or behave in ways that are incongruent with the paradigm, they disengage the very people they want to engage in the process.

The British Airways Story

In the summer of 1994, Neil Robertson, principal human resources business manager at British Airways, was facing a problem. BA was about to embark on an organizational change initiative called Leadership 2000. To meet the goals of Leadership 2000, significant changes would be required of the HR function. "I remember being concerned that if a solution was devised by a small number of people in one small room, would it be the right solution, and even if it were the right solution, would they be capable of implementing it," recalls Robertson. Other leaders in the HR organization shared this concern. The HR leadership decided to use the Conference Model to engage the HR organization and its internal customers in redesigning the organization to meet the needs of the future. Since that time, the HR organization has continued to employ the engagement paradigm as it supports change throughout the entire BA organization.

Recently, I spoke with Neil about his experience in a wide-ranging conversation in which he shared what he has learned over the past five years.

We began by talking about boundaries. "I believe the concept of boundaries is brilliant. Boundary statements require leaders to think about what success is and what success is not before the start of a change process. If the boundary statements are too tight, they feed the idea that everything is predetermined. On the other hand, if the boundary statements are too big, they can overload the process. It is similar to putting too many people on an elevator: if there are too many passengers, you can enter free fall. A boundary statement provides the answer to people who say that, in high-engagement processes, managers give up their authority and responsibility. What actually happens is that the managerial focus shifts from micro managing the details to ensuring that a set of boundary conditions are met."

Our conversation then shifted to widening the circle of involvement. "Widening the circle of involvement involves two things: increasing the *number* and the *diversity* of the people who are involved. When we redesigned HR, most of the people in the room were from HR and we had a smattering of line customers. I suspect the results might have been different had we had a larger number of line customers involved in the process. I think the result would have had more of a field orientation than the design that was eventually adopted. I think the choices about numbers and diversity of thought are critical. Numbers deal with creating a critical mass of people who are committed to implementing the outcomes, while diversity of thought shapes the result. Getting both numbers and diversity right is critical."

Neil went on to speak about the importance of start-up. "In the beginning, there needs to be informed consent by the leadership. They really need to understand the implications of what they are agreeing to do. It needs to be more than, 'This is a good process. Trust me.' They need to understand the potential, the risks, and the benefits. They need to be deeply involved in the boundary discussions, the number and diversity of people that will be involved in the process, and what it will take to maintain the operation while this change process is going on. Everyone who is going to be involved in the change process needs to understand why the change is necessary, the purpose—what we are trying to accomplish, and the level of engagement required. Recently, we started a change process with a two-day workshop whose only objective was to help understand what was happening in the world that necessitated this change."

"Universally we find that leaders always underestimate the time and attention the change process will require. I know in our own case that, when we reorganized HR, we spent a lot of time involving people from the very beginning, which for some made the design process longer than they thought it should be. However, we had a very rapid implementation as a result."

Neil also had some thoughts about the relationship between large group sessions and small group sessions. He came up with this guideline. "In situations where you have a small organization and a simple work process, then total involvement works. However, in situations where the system is large in numbers and complex, then a combination of large group sessions and small group sessions seems to be best. The large group is used to get a sense of direction and the small group to work out the details. We call these the macro and micro views. There is a tension between the macro and micro views. Sometimes the micro view fills in the details of the macro approach, and other times information gained when doing the micro work causes shifts in the macro approach. On other occasions, the macro view guides the work of the micro view. One thing I am sure of is that micro-failures are disastrous."

Building in short-term success is essential. Neil commented, "If you overload the change process and try to do too much, then the change process loses focus. People get discouraged because they do not see progress. I think it is far better to pull back on your goals and do something that can be readily achieved and develop a sense of accomplishment than to set as your goal a major transformation that takes so long that people lose focus and get frustrated because nothing is happening."

With regard to embracing democratic principles, Neil said, "The key here is that people need to be respected for their knowledge and contribution. If they do not feel respected, they disengage. Leaders have a high-level view of the work that is done in their organizations. However, they do not have a good understanding of the detail of what goes on. If you want to be successful in changing the way work is done, then you must involve, listen to, and respect the ideas and contributions of those doing the work. Along with involvement, transparency is essential. By transparency, I mean making everything visible. We have used displays and information boards as a way for people to both understand what was going on and to provide feedback."

Near the end of our conversation, Neil commented on what he saw as a byproduct of the engagement paradigm. "It is my belief that managers do not know it all and they have to find ways to tap into the knowledge of the organization. How to get the system talking to itself in useful and systematic ways is crucial to success. When we are successful, we find that, in addition to bringing about organizational change, we have increased the capacity of both leaders and their organizations to handle change. This may be the most important outcome of all."

Summary

Without careful application, engagement can disengage. This is the message of this chapter. The engagement shadow has three aspects: The leadership shadow includes conversational styles, discounting behaviors, and a failure to recognize organizational damage that can lead to disengagement. The strategy shadow involves manipulative strategies, unclear decision rules and boundaries, and violations of equity and fairness principles that also produce disengagement. And the engagement paradigm itself has a shadow side that can create disengagement—it is more chaotic than other paradigms, it requires leaders to let go of prerogatives, it requires a higher initial investment, and it is highly visible, all of which can lead to trouble if left unattended.

8

The Power of Engagement

The engagement paradigm is a powerful alternative to today's approaches to organizational change. Instead of increasing cynicism and resistance to manipulation, the engagement paradigm produces organizations in which people understand the issues and are ready and willing to act. Organizations that use the engagement paradigm develop the capacity not only to address current issues but to meet future challenges as well.

Today many leaders recognize that waterfall approaches to change and change processes that require intricate committee structures take too long. They also know that enthusiasm for any change diminishes the further one is from the inception of the change process. For leaders frustrated with current processes, leaders who know that something is missing, the engagement paradigm provides a robust alternative. It speeds implementation because a critical mass of people is involved from the very beginning, and produces high-quality solutions with high degrees of ownership and commitment as well.

Review

It's useful to pause for a quick review of the key aspects before taking a look at what this new paradigm has to offer in today's complex business environment. To achieve the promise of the engagement paradigm, leaders must incorporate the four essential tenets: widening the circle of involvement, connecting people to each other and ideas, creating communities for action, and embracing democratic principles.

Widening the circle of involvement from the very beginning speeds implementation because it increases ownership and eliminates the need to sell a decision created by others. When we widen the circle of involvement, we create a critical mass of champions who support the change process. Widening the circle has the additional benefits of increasing adaptation, innovation, and learning. The challenge for leaders is not just to include more people than ever before but to include people with more diverse points of view, bringing those who are not necessarily predisposed to agree with them into the process along with those who like the idea from the first.

Having widened the circle, the challenge is to create connections between people and ideas. This means working together to create a compelling purpose. In doing so, it is critical to honor the past as you create the future. Respecting the work and effort that has preceded the current need for change reduces blame and militates against the perception that this process is just another "flavor of the month." Connecting people to each other occurs when we bring the various parts of the system together so that they can talk to each other and learn how the whole system works. Connections across organizational boundaries are created as people work together to identify possibilities for the future. Taking the time to build relationships between people and ideas is essential to creating necessary connections.

The next challenge leaders face is to create a community that is ready to act from this enlarged group of connected people. Caring is a function of consent, not control. Therefore, the challenge for leaders is how to create a community of people who care about the outcomes within institutions that are predicated on order, control, and predictability. This occurs when leaders create conditions that demonstrate that each member of the community is valued. In doing so, leaders must make room for celebrating successes and learning from the failures that occur during any change process. To sustain commitment, it is essential to create information-sharing and feedback systems so that community members can monitor progress. Mutual support must be built into the process. Finally, it is essential that leaders be fully engaged in the change process and model behaviors that are congruent with the proposed changes.

Perhaps the most difficult challenge leaders face is embracing democratic principles. Leaders who employ the engagement paradigm all describe it as a profound process of letting go as they share information, power, and prerogatives with the organization. It leads to high anxiety and sleepless nights as leaders learn to stay with uncertainty as they bet on self-management and the organization's ability to resolve complex issues. Creating a safe enough environment, developing equity and fairness, allowing high-involvement decision making, and promoting freedom and autonomy are the important challenges that leaders face as they embrace democratic principles.

I have presented the four principles as if they were independent and could be met one at a time. The reality is that they are interconnected and must be met simultaneously. This perhaps is the biggest challenge of all, requiring courage, vulnerability, patience, persistence, and personal engagement. It is no small task. However, leaders who have persevered to see the process through readily attest to its value.

Eight Issues Facing Business Organizations Today

It is apparent to me that there are at least eight chronic issues facing organizations today for which the engagement paradigm provides an effective alternative:

- The sheer volume of change
- The introduction of new technology
- The trend toward mergers, acquisitions, and alliances
- The need to support innovation, adaptation, and learning
- The dissociation of people from communities
- The move from static to dynamic systems
- The development of organizational learning
- The rise of authoritarian behavior

I am calling these issues *chronic* because of our inability to resolve them effectively and conclusively: we think that we have resolved them only to have them reappear again and again.

Volume of Change

The sheer volume of change present in organizations today is cause for concern. There is usually more than one change effort going on in an organization at any given time. It is not uncommon for an organization to be introducing new technology that affects roles and relationships, and redesigning organizational structures, and at the same time attempting to change the organization's culture. It is also not uncommon to have different consultants for these different efforts, each with a pet theory of how the change process should unfold—with protocols ranging from highly bureaucratic to highly participative. The resulting chaos is predictable. These multiple change efforts, with their differing goals, sponsors, advisers, and approaches, with little communication and coordination between them, leave organization members confused about direction and expected outcomes.

Reflect for a moment what a difference it would make if all change processes in an organization followed the principles of the engagement paradigm. In addition to helping develop a common approach and identify a common set of values, the engagement paradigm can coordinate these diversified change processes with a common set of actions. Indeed, the future of the engagement paradigm may be to become the "killer app" of change processes. (A *killer app* is a software program that supersedes and coordinates other programs.)

New Technologies

We are missing the boat when we use change management processes to introduce new technology. Often the goal of these change processes is to control the resistance that accompanies the introduction of the technology. The engagement paradigm can effect far greater results than a mere managing of resistance; it can increase ownership and improve the quality of the system itself as large numbers of people work side by side with system planners to design new programs and identify potential pitfalls.

However, there is a more far-reaching benefit. Introducing new technology profoundly changes the way people work. Information is increased, jobs change, roles and relationships are rearranged. When we introduce new information systems, we tend to place huge amounts of attention on what appears on the screen and very little on the impact of this change on jobs, roles, and relationships.

The introduction of the assembly line largely ignored the impact on individuals and working relationships, relegating people to "just doing their part," and I believe that today's technological revolution is making the same mistake. New information systems are changing both the way work is done and the amount of information available to individuals. Killer apps, enterprise resource programs, and other information systems shift not only the way we work but also our work roles, responsibilities, and relationships. And yet we typically introduce such technology with little regard for its impact on people, involving them only when it comes time to implement the new system. The engagement paradigm provides a powerful alternative: it can be used to create new organizational structures and to clarify roles, responsibilities, and relationships so that the benefits of the new technology can achieve their full promise.

Technology is democratizing the workplace by making more information available than ever before, yet top-down management styles and silo organizations prevent people from using this information effectively. What good does it do to provide people with information and then limit their ability to act? The engagement paradigm supports providing people with the freedom they need to use the information that is now available.

As in the example from the Air Force base in Chapter Three, the engagement paradigm can powerfully influence the introduction of new technologies. In this example, the engagement paradigm did not appear on the scene until after the technological changes were already designed. Imagine what might have happened if the engagement paradigm had been used to introduce new technology from the very beginning, thereby deeply engaging people in the design of the technological improvements and the ensuing changes in roles and responsibilities.

Mergers, Acquisitions, and Alliances

Mergers and acquisitions are now a global phenomenon and, more often than not, they have clear winners and losers. They provide fertile ground for the engagement paradigm, which can be used to create a new organizational culture that is more effective than the original cultures of the merged or acquired companies. The paradigm can be used to address the following issues: How do we engage people who work in organizations halfway around the world? How do we integrate the work processes of these new organizations? How do we allow for the subtleties of cultures of people from different countries and different organizations within the context of a single organizational culture? How do we create an organizational culture that spans countries, language, and custom? How do we prevent the loss of each culture's uniqueness in the process?

Connected to the issue of mergers and acquisitions is the issue of alliances. Today many former competitors are forming alliances to meet the demands of an increasingly complex market. This requires processes for creating teamwork and cooperation that span organizational policies, procedures, and cultures. In these situations, the engagement paradigm can be used to create or strengthen the alliance by involving people from all the organizations to develop a compelling purpose, identify roles and responsibilities, create powerful working relationships, and—along with customers, suppliers, and important others—create unique products and services.

Inova Health System (Chapter Two) and Mercy Healthcare (Chapter Three) provide examples of how the Engagement Paradigm can be used in mergers, acquisitions, and alliances. In these cases, in addition to the process improvements that were developed by means of the paradigm, a new organizational identity emerged. Participants' primary identity shifted from their hospital location to the larger organization. Instead of identifying themselves as employees of a particular hospital, they would call themselves members of the "Inova system" or the "Mercy system." Chapter Three also describes an alliance my colleagues and I formed with two other consulting firms to create a joint workshop. Our experience there supports the value of the engagement paradigm in developing alliances. Following its principles helped to us to form an alliance that worked, create a new and exciting offer, and identify how the profits would be shared in a fair and equitable manner.

Supporting Innovation, Adaptation, and Learning

Throughout this book you have seen examples of how innovation, adaptation, and learning were increased through use of the engagement paradigm—from directory assistance operators developing new procedures to resolve long-standing issues to nurses discovering more efficient and caring ways of treating patients. Innovation, adaptation, and learning occurred because when the circle of involvement widens, variety enters the system. It is this variety of people and ideas that increases the probability that innovation, adaptation, and learning will occur.

I do not believe that modern business can continue the cycle of engaging people in fabulous off-site events where there is free-flowing information and collaboration across organizational units only to have them return to organizational structures that support limited information flow and provincialism. In today's fast-paced business environment, we must have organizational structures that support innovation, adaptation, and learning. Without these changes, we will never completely realize the benefits of the engagement paradigm. My group's work with the Conference Model has proven that it is possible to engage large numbers of people in the redesign of their organizations. The goals of many of these redesign efforts have been to improve efficiency, customer service, and quality. But the engagement paradigm can also be used to create organizations that foster innovation, are able to adapt to rapidly changing environments, and are able to learn from their experiences.

Dissociation from Communities

The communities in which we live also give us cause for concern. We are seeing an increasing dissociation of people from their communities and the governments that serve them. We live in communities in which no one knows anyone else's name and we become involved in them only when something happens in our own back yard. Reengaging people in their communities and governments is critical. Many local governments and private foundations are struggling with this issue. Future Search Associates is a group of consultants who conduct Future Search Conferences to help communities, schools, social service agencies, and other not-for-profit organizations engage stakeholders in creating viable futures. Developed by Marvin Weisbord and Sandra Janoff, the Future Search Conference is a forerunner to the engagement paradigm, and has been used around the world.

In 1998, Kuhuku Hospital, a rural community hospital located on Hawaii's north shore, was on life support: its ability to continue to provide basic health services to the community was very much in doubt. One year later, the hospital is breathing on its own. That year, along with Sandra Janoff, I conducted a conference based on the engagement paradigm to determine the hospital's future. The conference opened to ancient drumming and dancing. During the conference those assembled were linked to the island's history and to the hospital's beginnings as a sugar plantation medical facility. The participants also learned of the hard, cold economics that threatened to close the hospital, and explored the importance of the survival of this hospital to the community. One year later it celebrated its fiftieth anniversary thanks to the support of local citizens, health care providers, physicians, private foundations, and even competing medical institutions.

Moving from Static to Dynamic Systems

Another issue is the move from static to dynamic systems. Whether it was ever true is doubtful, but there was a time when we believed that we could change things once and they would be fixed forever. We now know that the only constant is change. It used to be that we were members of one organizational team and we only had to concern ourselves with making that team effective. Now people find themselves working on many teams with different agendas and purposes. The engagement paradigm will help us to move beyond team building to creating team-based cultures in which people will have multiple team memberships, have different roles in different teams, and be able to move in and out of teams with ease.

Organizational Learning

The other day, I visited the school where my daughter, Heather, teaches kindergarten. What stood out to me from my tour of the school was the classroom setup. Instead of desks and chairs in orderly rows facing the teacher, tables and chairs were arranged so that children could interact with one another. Students are learning to work together as they study and learn. They are learning essential skills for the future. There is hope.

Is it possible to create learning organizations in today's fast-paced environment? Do we have the will to take time out for the necessary reflection that is at the heart of such an endeavor? Can we sit with others and reflect on what is working and not working in our organizations today? Can we give each other the gift of thoughtful discourse? Or will our desire for speed kill learning?

The large group sessions that are part of the engagement paradigm can provide a forum in which organizations can begin to learn how to learn. In these sessions, organization members come together and ask the essential questions: What is working? What is not working? What do we need to do differently? In this way, learning is being incorporated into the fabric of the organization, not relegated to the classroom or some post-activity report.

A major bank conducted a large group learning session in an effort to consolidate its experience with reengineering. Participants from various organizations that had undergone reengineering along with the consultants engaged in a two-day session for sharing learning and thinking about the future. Before this, there were a variety of privately held opinions about the reengineering, but there was little collective wisdom. This large group session based on the engagement paradigm changed all that by sharing common experiences of what worked, what did not work, and what to do differently in the future.

Rise of Authoritarian Behavior

Will our desire for speed and instant answers give rise to a whole new era of authoritarian behavior? Will the need for immediate action become the excuse for disengaging the organization? Will we return to authoritarianism because we are too busy to care? Game theory makes it clear that, in the short run, those who take a win-lose strategy will always win over those employing a win-win strategy. However, organizations that develop a win-win culture will always do better in the long run.

One of the greatest fears expressed at the outset of any change process is, Will the leadership be here to see the process through, or will a new leader come in and disrupt everything that we have accomplished? Will a new leader come in and operate from a win-lose perspective after we have worked so hard to build teamwork and cooperation? The engagement paradigm can be used to create cultures in which win-lose behaviors are not tolerated, cultures that are strong enough not to be overturned by the whim of new leaders. Thus the engagement paradigm is an essential mechanism for maintaining organizational change.

Some Closing Thoughts

It's not too late to begin. You need not use the engagement paradigm from the very beginning of your change process in order to achieve powerful results. My colleagues and I have successfully helped organizations switch to the engagement paradigm from other paradigms. Remember the Detroit Edison example? This is a tricky process, but it is possible. The important thing to remember is how to honor and integrate the work that has preceded the move to the engagement paradigm.

A New Model for Organizations

For the past five years, I have been involved with the School for Managing, a unique approach to management education. This school, founded by Peter Block and the Association for Quality and Participation, is unique in today's world because it engages the participants in their own learning as it seeks to build bridges between the for-profit and not-for-profit world. It goes against current thinking because it goes for depth instead of the short course, each class meeting in eight three-day sessions over the course of nine months. At the school, both faculty and students are learners. The school seeks to explore and understand the tension between four critical factors in organizations today, as shown in Figure 8-1.

This model demonstrates the dynamic tension in organizations today. The vertical tension is between purpose and form. Do the organizational forms (structures, policies, procedures, and means of engagement) fit the purpose? The horizontal tension is between individual freedom and community. In today's organizations, we must balance the need for individual autonomy and control and the

Figure 8-1 Four Critical Factors

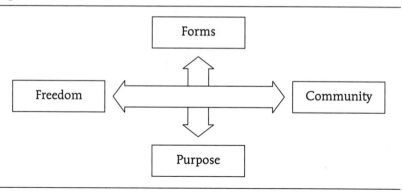

needs of the larger community that makes up the organization. Most organizational change efforts focus primarily on form, or changing the organization's structure, and pay scant attention to the issues of purpose, freedom, and community. When organizations use the engagement paradigm, they cannot run away from these quintessential issues. Instead, they meet them head on, but with powerful results.

The Importance of Individual Behavior

Personal behavior profoundly influences others. Do not take it lightly, as its power cannot be underestimated. In *The Reader,* Bernard Schlink sums it up in one simple but powerful phrase:
 "The truth of what one says lies in what one does."
 Remember this always and let it guide your actions.
 Let me end with one last story.

First Union Mortgage Corporation: The Florida Story

In one of the world's largest financial services organizations, business unit boundaries and reporting structures seem to be constantly shifting. Managers and team members at all levels must adapt and thrive within a changing environment. Within this environment, the mortgage lending (sales and operations) organization has built an adaptive, team-driven culture through the use of large conference methods for redesigning the organization and implementing new processes and structures. The organization currently spans thirteen states, employs over fifteen hundred people, and is continuously re-defining and improving its partnerships with other company divisions and subsidiaries.

Two years after first employing large conference methods to re-design and reorganize the organization into a team-based structure, the mortgage lending division faced a critical challenge. In what amounted to an "internal merger," the organization was asked to blend its sales and operations efforts with another mortgage group, managed separately by the largest "state bank" in the corporation. This decision was made at the highest corporate levels with the aim of reducing fragmentation and finding efficiencies within the corporation. The state organization would now have to integrate its operations with the larger mortgage subsidiary.

News of the decision sent shock waves throughout the state organization. The state had operated for decades as a traditional mortgage bank, with its own way of doing business. Like many lending institutions, strong rifts existed between field salespeople and their central-ized service team counterparts. The servicenters themselves were organized by function, with separate areas for processing applications, making credit decisions, and closing and funding mortgage loans. This turf-supporting structure had created headaches for customers, em-ployees, and senior executives for years and years. Nonetheless, resis-tance to changing the system was high, a sentiment made worse because changes were about to be imposed by "outsiders."

Change was indeed on the way, and most people in the state organization expected the worst. Two of three servicenters would be closed and employees at those sites would be asked to take on other roles within the parent company. Jobs and whole functions in the remaining servicenter would be redesigned so that everyone faced new roles and new work flows. All of this would have to happen within sixty to ninety days before the spring home buying season hit so that newly formed teams could successfully handle the certain spike in volume. Skepticism could not have been higher, nor morale lower.

The mortgage organization's leadership knew that team members throughout the state would have to be engaged in creating as much of their own future as possible if commitment and ownership were to be gained. Within the parameters of certain "givens"—decisions that had already been made at the corporate level and would not be changed—a *transition team* of key stakeholders from the many areas involved was formed to craft a process for moving into the new organization. An internal consultant worked with this team over a thirty-day period to build a strategy for engagement and change.

The centerpiece of the change effort was a series of two-day conferences in which newly announced service teams assembled for the first time, together with their sales counterparts, to jointly plan their future. The purpose of these conferences was twofold:

- To build stronger relationships and a sense of common customer ownership between the sales and service units.
- To work out details within the cross-functional service teams related to work processes, roles, resources, interteam relationships, and so on.

The first order of business was to eliminate the emotional baggage and soften the extreme *"us versus them"* perceptions that existed between the sales and service team members. As participants entered the room prior to the conference kickoff, some people actually resisted being asked to sit at the same table with their cross-team counterparts. Many of these people had worked and fought for years, by phone and by fax, without ever meeting in person. They expected fireworks and dreaded what was sure to be an uncomfortable showdown.

In small mixed groups, sales and service team members began by connecting at a personal level. They shared personal stories and challenges. They compared notes on positive and regrettable customer interactions. They shared misunderstandings about their own group that they wanted to clear up. They were asked to take personal risks by naming their own contribution to the negative patterns, and what they might do differently to improve the situation. Over the course of Day 1 the sense of dread and tension gave way to a powerful sense of shared challenge and identity. This served as a foundation for efforts to come.

Next came the daunting task of thinking through process coordination and role issues so that the coming customer wave could be handled with success. The starting point for this work was a full conference review of the overall mortgage origination process that both sales and service units had to jointly understand and own. This gave everyone a greater awareness of how the whole system fit together and where key interdependencies were located. Then sales and service teams, grouped in new regional assignments, slogged through tough questions about how customer handoffs should work in the future. They worked out how resources and information would be shared, what each unit expected of the other, and how they would continue to build on their growing common ground. Team plans were shared in full conference. The teams "stole" the best ideas from each other and identified and resolved organization-level issues that required full community decision making.

By the end of Day 2, the teams left feeling hopeful, energized, and prepared to tackle the coming increase in volume. The change process was not finished—in fact, it was just beginning—but much of the skepticism and hostility was behind them. The primary sentiment was that "we are all in this together, we are all trying to make it work, and we will."

Three years later, the state mortgage organization is a resounding success story. The operation is handling greater volume with higher quality and reduced cycle times at lower costs. The division has been able to document a 25 percent reduction in the overall cost structure of the state mortgage operation. In addition, the servicenter was recently awarded "Servicenter of the Year" by the corporation for its improved customer service, quality, and efficiency. The current servicenter manager, who stepped into his challenging role just weeks after the merger was announced, refers to the conferences as a major reason for the success of the change process. "It was definitely the right way to go, to bring people face to face and get the tough issues out in the open for everyone to deal with. Otherwise they would have slugged it out behind the scenes and repeated the same old negative patterns. The conferences were a true turning point for us."

Conclusion

So here I am at the end of the book raising a whole new set of issues instead of tying things up in a neat package. This is the nature of change. You set off toward a goal, but as you approach that goal, a whole new set of possibilities and issues emerge. Just when you think you have the answer, new questions appear. Just when you think you have reached your destination, new challenges appear.

The journey that started when you picked up *Terms of Engagement: Changing the Way We Change Organizations* is ending. I hope that reading this book has stimulated your thinking about the nature of organizational change and your role in leading change. I am sure that we did not always agree. My wish is that, after reading this book, you think about change differently from the way you did before you began, and that you will be willing to try the concepts that I have outlined. I am very interested in hearing from you what works and what does not work. In this way, we will continue to refine and enhance the engagement paradigm. To facilitate dialogue and discussion, my colleagues and I have established a Web site at www.axelrodgroup.com. Please join us there to continue the discussion.

Bibliography

Argyris, Chris. *Overcoming Organizational Defenses: Facilitating Organizational Learning.* Needham Heights, Mass.: Allyn & Bacon, 1990.

Axelrod, Emily M., and Richard H. Axelrod. *The Conference Model.* San Francisco: Berrett-Koehler, 1999.

Axelrod, Robert, and Michael Cohen. *Harnessing Complexity: Organizational Implications of a Scientific Frontier.* New York: Free Press, forthcoming.

Bateson, Gregory. *Mind and Nature.* New York: Bantam Books, 1980.

Beckhard, Richard, and Reuben T. Harris. *Organizational Transitions: Managing Complex Change.* Reading, Mass.: Addison-Wesley, 1977.

Central Conference of American Rabbis. *Gates of Repentance: The New Union Prayerbook for the Days of Awe.* New York: Central Conference of American Rabbis, 1978.

Coch, Lester, and John R. P. French. "Overcoming Resistance to Change." *Human Relations* 1, 4 (1948): 512-532.

Cohen, Mitchell, and Nicole Fermon, eds. *Princeton Readings in Political Thought.* Princeton, N.J.: Princeton University Press, 1996.

Cornford, Francis MacDonald, trans. *The Republic of Plato.* New York: Oxford University Press, 1958.

Emery, F. E., and Trist, E. L. "Socio-Technical Systems." In C. W. Churchman and others (eds.), *Management Sciences, Models, and Techniques.* London: Pergamon, 1960.

Emery, Merrelyn, ed. *Participative Design for Participative Democracy.* Canberra: Centre for Continuing Education, Australian National University, 1993.

Fritz, Robert. *The Path of Least Resistance.* San Francisco: Berrett-Koehler, 1999.

Gardner, Howard. *Leading Minds: An Anatomy of Leadership.* New York: Basic Books, 1996.

Goleman, Daniel. *Emotional Intelligence: Why It Can Matter More Than IQ.* New York: Bantam Books, 1995.

Hausser, D. L., P. A. Pecorella, and A. L. Wissler. *Survey-Guided Development: A Manual for Consultants.* Ann Arbor: Institute for Social Research, University of Michigan, 1975.

Jacobi, Jolande. *The Psychology of C. G. Jung.* London: Yale University Press, 1973.

Kaplan, J. D., ed. *Dialogues of Plato.* New York: Washington Square Press, 1963.

Kotter, John P. *Leading Change.* Boston: Harvard Business School Press, 1996.

Kurtz, Ron. *Body-Centered Psychotherapy: The Hakomi Method.* Mendocino, Calif.: LifeRhythm, 1990.

Lindaman, E., and R. Lippitt. *Choosing the Future You Prefer: A Goal Setting Guide.* Ann Arbor, Mich.: Human Resource Development Associates of Ann Arbor, 1979.

Lewin, Kurt. *Resolving Social Conflicts: Selected Papers on Group Dynamics.* Edited by G. W. Lewin. New York: Harper & Row, 1948.

McGregor, D. *The Human Side of Enterprise.* New York: McGraw Hill, 1960.

McKnight, John. *The Careless Society: Community and Its Counterfeits.* New York: Basic Books, 1995.

McMaster, Michael D. *The Intelligent Advantage: Organizing for Complexity.* Boston: Butterworth-Heinemann, 1996.

Morgan, Gareth. *Images of Organization.* Newbury Park, Calif.: Sage, 1986.

Ornish, Dean. *Dr. Dean Ornish's Program for Reversing Heart Disease.* New York: Random House, 1990.

Owen, Harrison. *Open Space Technology: A User's Guide.* San Francisco: Berrett-Koehler, 1997.

Putnam, Robert D. "Bowling Alone: America's Declining Social Capital." *Journal of Democracy* 6, 1 (1995): 65-78.

Schlink, Bernhard. *The Reader.* New York: Vintage Books, 1995.

Senge, Peter M. *The Fifth Discipline: The Art and Practice of the Learning Organization.* New York: Doubleday, 1990.

Sherwood, John J. "Creating Work Cultures with Competitive Advantage." *Organizational Dynamics* (winter 1988): 5-27.

Shtogren, John A., ed. *Models for Management: The Structure of Competence.* The Woodlands, Tex.: Teleometrics International, 1980.

Somé, Malidoma Patrice. *Ritual: Power, Healing, and Community.* Portland: Swan/Rave, 1993.

Tannenbaum, Robert, and Warren H. Schmidt "How to Choose a Leadership Pattern." *Harvard Business Review* 51, 3 (May-June 1973): 162-189.

Taylor, Frederick W. *The Principles of Scientific Management.* New York: Harper & Row, 1915.

Vroom, Victor H., and Philip Yetton. *Leadership and Decision Making.* Pittsburgh: University of Pittsburgh Press, 1973.

Weisbord, Marvin R., and Sandra Janoff. *Future Search: An Action Guide to Finding Common Ground in Organizations and Communities.* San Francisco: Berrett-Koehler, 1995.

Zweig, Connie, and Jeremiah Abrams, ed. *Meeting the Shadow: The Hidden Power of the Dark Side of Human Nature.* Los Angeles: Tarcher, 1991.

Index

About the Author

Richard H. Axelrod helped to revolutionize the world of organizational change when, along with his wife Emily, he developed the Conference Model, a process for engaging an entire organization in systemwide change. Realizing that in today's world it is no longer acceptable for the few to meet behind closed doors and design for the many, Axelrod became a pioneer in the use of large groups to effect organizational change.

The Engagement Paradigm was born out of Richard's work on the Conference Model and his experience with other large group change methodologies. Emily's background as an educator and family therapist has deepened the paradigm.

Richard brings over twenty-five years of consulting and teaching experience with leading companies to this work. His clients include British Airways, Bell South, First Union Bank, Harley Davidson, Hewlett-Packard, Intel, and Mercy Healthcare Sacramento.

Richard is an active professional. Currently he is working with Peter Block and the Association for Quality and Participation to develop the School for Managing and Leading Change, an innovative approach to management education. Before forming The Axelrod Group, Inc., in 1981, Richard was an organization development manager for General Foods.

Richard and Emily co-authored *The Conference Model* and Richard is a contributing author to *Discovering Common Ground* by Weisbord and others, *The Change Handbook* by Devane and Holman, and *The Flawless Consulting Field Book* by Peter Block.

Richard received his MBA from the University of Chicago and lives with Emily in Wilmette, Illinois. Richard and Emily have two adult children; Heather Oliver, a kindergarten teacher in Dallas, Texas, and David Axelrod, a professional ski instructor in Breckenridge, Colorado.

Richard can be reached at The Axelrod Group, 723 Laurel Avenue, Wilmette IL 60091, by phone at 877-233-8054, or at www.axelrodgroup.com on the World Wide Web.

About The Axelrod Group

The Axelrod Group, Inc., is a Chicago-based consulting firm with affiliates throughout the United States and Europe. It specializes in consulting to companies and nonprofit institutions that wish to engage their organizations in addressing critical issues such as strategic initiatives; mergers, acquisitions, and alliances; new technology implementation; organization and process redesign; and the creation of team-based structures.

The Axelrod Group provides two types of training based on the engagement paradigm. The first is the Conference Model seminar. In a highly stimulating learning environment participants immerse themselves in a powerful simulation that drives home the principles of the engagement paradigm. Workshop participants experience the power of the engagement paradigm as they learn to apply the Conference Model process to the redesign of organizations and processes.

The second offering, *The Essential Skills of Engaging and Convening Workshop,* is for teams charged with the responsibility for bringing about organizational change. In this workshop, intact teams from different organizations come together to develop an overall change strategy and specific interventions based on the principles of the engagement paradigm. A distinctive feature of this workshop is that consultants from VISTA Consulting Team Ltd., Robert Jacobs Consulting, and other firms join consultants from The Axelrod Group. Each firm has its own perspective on engagement; consequently, participant teams are introduced to a variety of viewpoints, perspectives, case studies, and practices. Participant teams leave the workshop having

developed a customized change strategy that fits their unique circumstances, is grounded in the principles of the engagement paradigm, and is strengthened by their interaction with teams from other
organizations.

The Axelrod Group has a variety of videos describing their work.
For the latest copies, or to obtain other information, please contact

The Axelrod Group, Inc.
723 Laurel Avenue
Wilmette, IL 60091
877-233-8054
www.axelrodgroup.com